Elizabeth Job

I1009833

COLLINS
POCKET
FRENCH
VERB TABLES

HarperCollins*Publishers*

First published in this edition 1993

© **HarperCollins Publishers** 1993

ISBN 0 00 470154-2

---

editor
Lesley A Robertson

editorial management
Vivian Marr

editorial staff
Megan Maxwell

---

*A catalogue record for this book
is available from the British Library*

Typeset by Tradespools Ltd, Frome, Somerset

*Printed in Great Britain by
HarperCollins Manufacturing, Glasgow*

INTRODUCTION

Your **Collins Pocket French Verb Tables** is a handy quick-reference guide to one of the most important aspects of the French language. All the essential information about French verbs and how to use them is covered and the innovative use of colour throughout the text makes learning verb endings and irregularities easy – and fast!

The book is divided into three sections. The first section gives a detailed explanation of each of the three French verb conjugations, showing the regular endings in each conjugation for all the main tenses, along with instructions on how to form the present participle, the past participle and the imperative in each conjugation. Compound tenses are explained in full, as is the use of the passive. Defective verbs and 'regular' spelling irregularities are listed and the glossary on page 9 gives invaluable help in describing the major verb categories.

The second section – the main part of the book – shows, in alphabetical order, each of 112 verb models, fully conjugated. Each verb model is clearly laid out across two pages with the learning points highlighted in colour – no more searching for where the stem ends and the ending begins. You can see at a glance which verb ending to use for which tense and which person. Major constructions and idiomatic phrases are given for most verb models and similarly conjugated verbs are listed, with their translations, for numerous verb types.

Finally, the third section of the book is an alphabetical index of over 2,000 common verbs, each one cross-referred to its basic model.

CONTENTS

THE FRENCH VERB

The majority of verbs are regular and conform to rules; the fact that irregular verbs do not follow any overall pattern means that they have to be learned individually.

The infinitive ending of regular verbs indicates to which conjugation or group they belong:

1st   conjugation: ER ending; model: DONNER (36)★
2nd   conjugation: IR ending; model: FINIR (45)★
3rd   conjugation: RE ending; model VENDRE (107)★
(★ = verb model number, not page number)

To conjugate a regular verb, you must add the appropriate verb ending to the appropriate tense stem. The stem for the present, imperfect, past historic and both subjunctive tenses is the infinitive minus its ER, IR or RE ending; the stem for the future and conditional tenses is the whole infinitive in the 1st and 2nd conjugations, and the infinitive minus its final E in the 3rd conjugation.

For each conjugation, the following tables show
   (1) the verb endings for each tense
   (2) how these are added to the stem.

Pr = present; I = imperfect; F = future; C = conditional; PH = past historic; PrS = present subjunctive; PS = past subjunctive

1st conjugation (1)

Tense	Endings					
Pr	e	es	e	ons	ez	ent
I	ais	ais	ait	ions	iez	aient
F	ai	as	a	ons	ez	ont
C	ais	ais	ait	ions	iez	aient
PH	ai	as	a	âmes	âtes	èrent
PrS	e	es	e	ions	iez	ent
PS	asse	asses	ât	assions	assiez	assent

4

	STEM	Pr	I	PH	Pr S	P S
je	**donn**	e	ais	ai	e	asse
tu	**donn**	es	ais	as	es	asses
il	**donn**	e	ait	a	e	ât
nous	**donn**	ons	ions	âmes	ions	assions
vous	**donn**	ez	iez	âtes	iez	assiez
ils	**donn**	ent	aient	èrent	ent	assent

	STEM	F	C
je	**donner**	ai	ais
tu	**donner**	as	ais
il	**donner**	a	ait
nous	**donner**	ons	ions
vous	**donner**	ez	iez
ils	**donner**	ont	aient

2nd conjugation (1)

Tense	Endings					
Pr	is	is	it	issons	issez	issent
I	issais	issais	issait	issions	issiez	issaient
F	ai	as	a	ons	ez	ont
C	ais	ais	ait	ions	iez	aient
PH	is	is	it	îmes	îtes	irent
PrS	isse	isses	isse	issions	issiez	issent
PS	isse	isses	it	issions	issiez	issent

(2)

	STEM	Pr	I	PH	Pr S	P S
je	**fin**	is	issais	is	isse	isse
tu	**fin**	is	issais	is	isses	isses
il	**fin**	it	issait	it	isse	ît
nous	**fin**	issons	issions	îmes	issions	issions
vous	**fin**	issez	issiez	îtes	issiez	issiez
ils	**fin**	issent	issaient	irent	issent	issent

	STEM	F	C
je	**finir**	**ai**	**ais**
tu	**finir**	**as**	**ais**
il	**finir**	**a**	**ait**
nous	**finir**	**ons**	**ions**
vous	**finir**	**ez**	**iez**
ils	**finir**	**ont**	**aient**

3rd conjugation (1)

Tense	*Endings*					
Pr	**s**	**s**	**—**	**ons**	**ez**	**ent**
I	**ais**	**ais**	**ait**	**ions**	**iez**	**aient**
F	**ai**	**as**	**a**	**ons**	**ez**	**ont**
C	**ais**	**ais**	**ait**	**ions**	**iez**	**aient**
PH	**is**	**is**	**it**	**îmes**	**îtes**	**irent**
PrS	**e**	**es**	**e**	**ions**	**iez**	**ent**
PS	**isse**	**isses**	**it**	**issions**	**issiez**	**issent**

(2)

	STEM	Pr	I	PH	PrS	PS
je	**vend**	**s**	**ais**	**is**	**e**	**isse**
tu	**vend**	**s**	**ais**	**is**	**es**	**isses**
il	**vend**		**ait**	**it**	**e**	**ît**
nous	**vend**	**ons**	**ions**	**îmes**	**ions**	**issions**
vous	**vend**	**ez**	**iez**	**îtes**	**iez**	**issiez**
ils	**vend**	**ent**	**aient**	**irent**	**ent**	**issent**

	STEM	F	C
je	**vendr**	**ai**	**ais**
tu	**vendr**	**as**	**ais**
il	**vendr**	**a**	**ait**
nous	**vendr**	**ons**	**ions**
vous	**vendr**	**ez**	**iez**
ils	**vendr**	**ont**	**aient**

THE PRESENT PARTICIPLE

To form the present participle, add the following endings to the infinitive minus its ER, IR or RE ending

    1st conjugation **ant**   (donnant)

    2nd conjugation **issant** (finissant)

    3rd conjugation **ant**   (vendant)

With the exception of 'en', French uses an infinitive after prepositions where English uses a present participle.

Thus: sans parler = without speaking

        après être parti = after having left

but: en faisant = while doing.

THE PAST PARTICIPLE

To form the past participle, add the following endings to the infinitive minus its ER, IR or RE ending

    1st conjugation **é** (donné)

    2nd conjugation **i**   (fini)

    3rd conjugation **u** (vendu)

For agreement rules in compound tenses, see p. 10.

THE IMPERATIVE

The imperative is the same as the present tense 'tu', 'nous' and 'vous' forms minus the subject pronouns: finis, allons, commencez.

Exceptions

1) ER verbs and verbs like cueillir, ouvrir etc, which keep the 's' ending of the 'tu' form only if it is immediately followed by y or en: avance, va; vas-y, cueilles-en.
2) avoir and être, whose imperative forms are the same as the present subjunctive (minus the 's' of 'tu' form for avoir).
3) vouloir: veuille, veuillons, veuillez.
4) savoir: sache, sachons, sachez.

Affirmative/negative imperative – pronoun object follows/precedes verb: prends-le/ne le prends pas; asseyez-vous/ne vous asseyez pas.

'REGULAR' SPELLING IRREGULARITIES

A number of spelling changes affect 1st conjugation verbs. Such changes and when they occur are shown below. Verb types are divided according to their infinitive ending. We suggest that you use the table in conjunction with the numbered verb models indicated. C = consonant(s).

-eler/-eter *(i: appeler 4/jeter 50;* *ii: acheter 1)* *either* i) l→ll/t→tt *or* ii) e→è	*before e, es, ent;* *throughout future and* *conditional tenses*
e + C + er *(lever 52)* e→è	*as above*
-éger *(protéger 80)* é→è; *see* **-ger**	*before e, es, ent;* *as for* **-ger**
-é + C + er *(espérer 41)* é→è	*before e, es, ent*
-oyer/-uyer *(nettoyer 63)* y→i	*before e, es, ent;* *throughout future and* *conditional tenses*
-ayer *(i: payer 70; ii: as for nettoyer* *63)* *either* i) y retained throughout *or* ii) y→i	*as above*
-cer *(commencer 15)* c→ç *(to soften c)*	*when verb endings* *starting with a or o* *immediately follow c*
-ger *(manger 54)* e retained *(to soften g)*	*when verb endings* *starting with a or o* *immediately follow g*

GLOSSARY

You should familiarize yourself with the following descriptions of major verb categories.

Transitive   taking a direct object
Intransitive   used without a direct object
★ A verb may be transitive in English yet intransitive in French (and vice versa):
  he disobeyed the rules (transitive)
  il a désobéi aux règles (intransitive)
  he looked at his sister (intransitive)
  il a regardé sa sœur (transitive)

Reflexive   taking a reflexive pronoun (English: myself, ourselves etc; French: me, nous etc) which 'reflects' back to the subject
★ 1) Not all verbs which are reflexive in French are reflexive in English
e.g. se coucher = to go to bed
   2) The reflexive pronoun is sometimes optional in English
     e.g. se laver = to wash (oneself)

Reciprocal   taking a reciprocal pronoun which expresses mutual action or relation
     e.g. ils se regardent = they look at each other *or* one another
★ Since the plural forms of reciprocal and reflexive verbs are identical, 'ils se regardent' might mean 'they look at themselves'. Always gauge the correct translation from the context.

Auxiliary   used to conjugate verbs in their compound tenses (see p. 10)

Impersonal   used only in the 3rd person singular, to represent a neutral subject
     e.g. il pleut = it's raining

9

COMPOUND TENSES: THE USE OF AUXILIARY VERBS

In simple tenses, the verb is expressed in one word (e.g. donne, finira, vendions); in compound tenses, the past participle is added to the appropriate tense of the auxiliary verbs avoir and être (e.g. a donné, aura fini, avions vendu). Most verbs are conjugated with avoir, but the être auxiliary is used with reflexive and reciprocal verbs, and when the verb is in the passive voice. (See note on Passive: p. 12)

The following intransitive verbs are also conjugated with être:

aller	revenir	passer*
venir	retourner*	rester
entrer*	rentrer*	devenir
sortir*	monter*	naître
arriver	descendre*	mourir
partir	tomber	

(* = conjugated with avoir when transitive)

RULES OF AGREEMENT FOR PAST PARTICIPLES

(a) The past participle of a verb conjugated with être agrees in number and gender with its subject.

Thus: elle est partie = she left

   elle s'est souvenue[1] = she remembered

   ([1]typical of verbs which are reflexive in form but whose pronouns have no true reflexive value)

Exceptions: 1) reflexives 2) reciprocals

   e.g. 1) elle s'est lavée (transitive)

      elle s'est parlé (intransitive)

   2) ils se sont regardés (transitive)

      ils se sont parlé (intransitive)

   (Exceptions explained in (b))

(b) The past participle of a verb conjugated with avoir and of a transitive reflexive or reciprocal verb agrees in number and gender with its direct object, provided the direct object precedes the verb; otherwise, the past participle remains invariable.

Thus: je les ai vendus = I sold them
      elle s'est lavée = she washed
      ils se sont regardés = they looked at each other

but: j'ai vendu les sacs = I sold the bags
      elle s'est parlé = she talked to herself
      (s' = indirect object)
      ils se sont parlé = they talked to each other
      (se = indirect object)
      (*NB*: elle s'est lavé les mains = she washed her hands – no agreement since direct object (les mains) follows the verb and s' = indirect object)

Some intransitive verbs (e.g. coûter, peser etc) may be accompanied by a complement of price, weight etc. Do not mistake this for a direct object: the past participle remains invariable – 'les 5 F que ça m'a coûté = the 5 F it cost me'; 'les 3 kilos que le colis a pesé = the 3 kilos the parcel weighed'. Also invariable are the past participles of impersonal verbs – 'les accidents qu'il y a eu = the accidents there were'.

For verbal constructions of the type 'I saw her leave', 'she heard them being scolded' (verbs of perception), or 'he took us swimming', which are translated in French by a verb plus infinitive, the rules of agreement are as follows:
1) if the preceding direct object is the subject of the infinitive, the past participle agrees in number and gender with it:
      je l'ai vue partir = I saw her leave
      il nous a emmenés nager = he took us swimming
2) if the preceding direct object is the object of the infinitive, the past participle remains invariable:
      elle les a entendu gronder
      = she heard them being scolded.

In constructions such as 'laisser faire' where laisser is used in conjunction with an infinitive, the same rules apply:
1) je les ai laissés tomber = I dropped them
2) elle s'est laissé persuader = she let herself be persuaded.

When faire is used in this way, however, it contradicts the 1st rule: the past participle remains invariable in both cases:
1) la femme qu'il a fait venir = the women he sent for
2) la montre qu'il a fait réparer = the watch he (has) had repaired.

THE PASSIVE VOICE
A transitive verb is active when its subject performs the action (she disobeyed the rules) and passive when its subject receives the action (she was punished). In French, the passive is formed by adding the past participle to the appropriate tense of être: 'elle était punie = she was punished' (note agreement with subject).

(*NB*: do not confuse a passive verb with an intransitive verb, which can only be used in the active voice –
elle était allée = she had gone)

French does not use the passive as extensively as English, preferring
either 1) 'on': on m'a dit que ... = I was told that ...
or 2) a reflexive verb with an inanimate subject:
ce mot ne s'emploie plus = this word is no longer used.

Note
In the tables on the following pages these abbreviations are used.
qch   quelque chose
qn   quelqu'un
sb   somebody
sth   something

12

DEFECTIVE VERBS

Defective verbs have missing or obsolete parts. The forms shown below are those most likely to occur. Unless otherwise stated, the auxiliary verb (where applicable) is avoir.

1 Present Participle *2* Past Participle *3* Present *4* Imperfect
5 Future *6* Conditional *7* Past Historic *8* Present Subjunctive
9 Past Subjunctive

accroire en faire accroire
apparoir *3* il appert
béer *1* béant *3* il bée *4* il béait
choir (être) *2* chu *3* chois, chois, choit, choient *5* choirai *etc*
  6 choirais *etc 7* il chut *9* il chût
déchoir *2* déchu *3* déchois, déchois, déchoit, déchoyons,
  déchoyez, déchoient *5* déchoirai *etc 6* déchoirais *etc 7* déchus
  etc 8 déchoie *etc 9* déchusse *etc*
échoir (être) *1* échéant *2* échu *3* il échoit *5* il échoira *6* il
  échoirait *7* il échut *8* il échoie *9* il échût
faillir *1* faillant *2* failli *5* faillirai *etc 6* faillirais *etc 7* faillis *etc*
  NB: j'ai failli tomber = I nearly fell
gésir *1* gisant *3* gis, gis, gît, gisons, gisez *4* gisais *etc*
messeoir *1* messéant *3* il messied, ils messiéent *6* il messiérait,
  ils messiéraient
oindre *1* oignant *2* oint *3* il oint *4* il oignait
ouïr *2* ouï
paître *1* paissant *3* pais, pais, paît, paissons, paissez, paissent
  4 paissais *etc 5* paîtrai *etc 6* paîtrais *etc 8* paisse *etc*
poindre *2* point *3* il point *5* il poindra
repaître *like* **paître** *but also has 2* repu *7* repus *etc 9* repusse *etc*
seoir (= *to become*) *1* seyant *3* il sied, ils siéent *4* il seyait, ils
  seyaient *5* il siéra, ils siéront *6* il siérait, ils siéraient *8* il siée

1 acheter

to buy

also **congeler**
to freeze

PRESENT PARTICIPLE
achetant

déceler
to discover

PAST PARTICIPLE
acheté

geler
to freeze

PRESENT

j'	**achète**
tu	**achètes**
il	**achète**
nous	**achetons**
vous	**achetez**
ils	**achètent**

IMPERFECT

j'	**achetais**
tu	**achetais**
il	**achetait**
nous	**achetions**
vous	**achetiez**
ils	**achetaient**

FUTURE

j'	**achèterai**
tu	**achèteras**
il	**achètera**
nous	**achèterons**
vous	**achèterez**
ils	**achèteront**

IMPERATIVE

achète
achetons
achetez

CONDITIONAL

j'	**achèterais**
tu	**achèterais**
il	**achèterait**
nous	**achèterions**
vous	**achèteriez**
ils	**achèteraient**

14

haleter
to paint

peler
to peel

PAST HISTORIC		PRESENT SUBJUNCTIVE	
j'	**achet**ai	j'	**achèt**e
tu	**achet**as	tu	**achèt**es
il	**achet**a	il	**achèt**e
nous	**achet**âmes	nous	**achet**ions
vous	**achet**âtes	vous	**achet**iez
ils	**achet**èrent	ils	**achèt**ent

PERFECT		PAST SUBJUNCTIVE	
j'	**ai acheté**	j'	**achet**asse
tu	**as acheté**	tu	**achet**asses
il	**a acheté**	il	**achet**ât
nous	**avons acheté**	nous	**achet**assions
vous	**avez acheté**	vous	**achet**assiez
ils	**ont acheté**	ils	**achet**assent

CONSTRUCTIONS

acheter qch à qn   to buy sth from sb; to buy sth for sb
je le lui ai acheté   I bought it from him; I bought it for him
je le lui ai acheté 10 F   I bought it from him for 10 F

2 acquérir

to acquire

also **conquérir**
to conquer

PRESENT PARTICIPLE
acquérant

s'enquérir
to inquire

PAST PARTICIPLE
acquis

requérir
to require

PRESENT		IMPERFECT	
j'	**acquiers**	j'	**acquér**ais
tu	**acquiers**	tu	**acquér**ais
il	**acquiert**	il	**acquér**ait
nous	**acquér**ons	nous	**acquér**ions
vous	**acquér**ez	vous	**acquér**iez
ils	**acquièrent**	ils	**acquér**aient

FUTURE

j'	**acquerr**ai
tu	**acquerr**as
il	**acquerr**a
nous	**acquerr**ons
vous	**acquerr**ez
ils	**acquerr**ont

IMPERATIVE

acquiers
acquérons
acquérez

CONDITIONAL

j'	**acquerr**ais
tu	**acquerr**ais
il	**acquerr**ait
nous	**acquerr**ions
vous	**acquerr**iez
ils	**acquerr**aient

PAST HISTORIC		*PRESENT SUBJUNCTIVE*	
j'	acquis	j'	acquière
tu	acquis	tu	acquières
il	acquit	il	acquière
nous	acquîmes	nous	**acquérions**
vous	acquîtes	vous	**acquériez**
ils	acquirent	ils	acquièrent

PERFECT		*PAST SUBJUNCTIVE*	
j'	**ai** acquis	j'	acquisse
tu	**as** acquis	tu	acquisses
il	**a** acquis	il	acquit
nous	**avons** acquis	nous	acquissions
vous	**avez** acquis	vous	acquissiez
ils	**ont** acquis	ils	acquissent

CONSTRUCTIONS

acquérir de l'expérience   to gain experience
acquérir de la valeur   to go up in value
les mauvaises habitudes s'acquièrent facilement   bad
habits are easily picked up

3 aller

to go

PRESENT PARTICIPLE
allant

PAST PARTICIPLE
allé

PRESENT

je	**vais**
tu	**vas**
il	**va**
nous	**all**ons
vous	**all**ez
ils	**vont**

IMPERFECT

j'	**all**ais
tu	**all**ais
il	**all**ait
nous	**all**ions
vous	**all**iez
ils	**all**aient

FUTURE

j'	**irai**
tu	**iras**
il	**ira**
nous	**irons**
vous	**irez**
ils	**iront**

IMPERATIVE

va
allons
allez

CONDITIONAL

j'	**irais**
tu	**irais**
il	**irait**
nous	**irions**
vous	**iriez**
ils	**iraient**

PAST HISTORIC		*PRESENT SUBJUNCTIVE*	
j'	**all**ai	j'	**aille**
tu	**all**as	tu	**aille**s
il	**all**a	il	**aille**
nous	**all**âmes	nous	**all**ions
vous	**all**âtes	vous	**all**iez
ils	**all**èrent	ils	**aille**nt

PERFECT		*PAST SUBJUNCTIVE*	
je	suis **allé**	j'	**all**asse
tu	es **allé**	tu	**all**asses
il	est **allé**	il	**all**ât
nous	sommes **allés**	nous	**all**assions
vous	êtes **allé(s)**	vous	**all**assiez
ils	sont **allés**	ils	**all**assent

CONSTRUCTIONS

aller faire qch   to go and do sth
aller à qn   to fit sb; to suit sb
comment allez-vous? – je vais bien/mal/mieux   how are you? – I'm well/unwell/better
s'en aller   to go (away); to leave
allons-y!   let's go!

4 appeler
to call

also amonceler
to pile up

PRESENT PARTICIPLE
appelant

épeler
to spell

PAST PARTICIPLE
appelé

jumeler
to twin

PRESENT
j'	**appel**le
tu	**appel**les
il	**appel**le
nous	**appel**ons
vous	**appel**ez
ils	**appel**lent

IMPERFECT
j'	**appel**ais
tu	**appel**ais
il	**appel**ait
nous	**appel**ions
vous	**appel**iez
ils	**appel**aient

FUTURE
j'	**appel**lerai
tu	**appel**leras
il	**appel**lera
nous	**appel**lerons
vous	**appel**lerez
ils	**appel**leront

IMPERATIVE
	appelle
	appelons
	appelez

CONDITIONAL
j'	**appel**lerais
tu	**appel**lerais
il	**appel**lerait
nous	**appel**lerions
vous	**appel**leriez
ils	**appel**leraient

rappeler
to recall

to call

renouveler
to renew

PAST HISTORIC		*PRESENT SUBJUNCTIVE*	
j'	appelai	j'	appelle
tu	appelas	tu	appelles
il	appela	il	appelle
nous	appelâmes	nous	appelions
vous	appelâtes	vous	appeliez
ils	appelèrent	ils	appellent
PERFECT		*PAST SUBJUNCTIVE*	
j'	ai appelé	j'	appelasse
tu	as appelé	tu	appelasses
il	a appelé	il	appelât
nous	avons appelé	nous	appelassions
vous	avez appelé	vous	appelassiez
ils	ont appelé	ils	appelassent

CONSTRUCTIONS
comment vous appelez-vous?   what's your name?
je m'appelle Suzanne   my name is Suzanne
appeler qn à l'aide *or* **au secours**   to call to sb for help
en appeler à   to appeal to

5 apprendre
to learn

PRESENT PARTICIPLE
apprenant

PAST PARTICIPLE
appris

PRESENT			*IMPERFECT*	
j'	**apprends**		j'	apprenais
tu	**apprends**		tu	apprenais
il	**apprend**		il	apprenait
nous	**apprenons**		nous	apprenions
vous	**apprenez**		vous	appreniez
ils	**apprennent**		ils	apprenaient

FUTURE	
j'	**apprendrai**
tu	**apprendras**
il	**apprendra**
nous	**apprendrons**
vous	**apprendrez**
ils	**apprendront**

IMPERATIVE		*CONDITIONAL*	
apprends		j'	**apprendrais**
apprenons		tu	**apprendrais**
apprenez		il	**apprendrait**
		nous	**apprendrions**
		vous	**apprendriez**
		ils	**apprendraient**

PAST HISTORIC		PRESENT SUBJUNCTIVE	
j'	appris	j'	apprenne
tu	appris	tu	apprennes
il	apprit	il	apprenne
nous	apprîmes	nous	apprenions
vous	apprîtes	vous	appreniez
ils	apprirent	ils	apprennent
PERFECT		**PAST SUBJUNCTIVE**	
j'	**ai** appris	j'	apprisse
tu	**as** appris	tu	apprisses
il	**a** appris	il	apprît
nous	**avons** appris	nous	apprissions
vous	**avez** appris	vous	apprissiez
ils	**ont** appris	ils	apprissent

CONSTRUCTIONS

apprendre à faire qch to learn (how) to do sth
apprendre qch à qn to teach sb sth; to tell sb sth
apprendre à qn à faire qch to teach sb (how) to do sth
l'espagnol s'apprend facilement Spanish is easy to learn

6 arriver
to arrive

PRESENT PARTICIPLE
arrivant

PAST PARTICIPLE
arrivé

PRESENT		*IMPERFECT*	
j'	**arriv**e	j'	**arriv**ais
tu	**arriv**es	tu	**arriv**ais
il	**arriv**e	il	**arriv**ait
nous	**arriv**ons	nous	**arriv**ions
vous	**arriv**ez	vous	**arriv**iez
ils	**arriv**ent	ils	**arriv**aient

		FUTURE	
		j'	**arriv**erai
		tu	**arriv**eras
		il	**arriv**era
		nous	**arriv**erons
		vous	**arriv**erez
		ils	**arriv**eront

IMPERATIVE		*CONDITIONAL*	
	arrive	j'	**arriv**erais
	arrivons	tu	**arriv**erais
	arrivez	il	**arriv**erait
		nous	**arriv**erions
		vous	**arriv**eriez
		ils	**arriv**eraient

PAST HISTORIC		PRESENT SUBJUNCTIVE	
j'	arrivai	j'	arrive
tu	arrivas	tu	arrives
il	arriva	il	arrive
nous	arrivâmes	nous	arrivions
vous	arrivâtes	vous	arriviez
ils	arrivèrent	ils	arrivent

PERFECT		PAST SUBJUNCTIVE	
je	suis arrivé	j'	arrivasse
tu	es arrivé	tu	arrivasses
il	est arrivé	il	arrivât
nous	sommes arrivés	nous	arrivassions
vous	êtes arrivé(s)	vous	arrivassiez
ils	sont arrivés	ils	arrivassent

CONSTRUCTIONS

arriver à faire qch   to succeed in doing sth
ça peut arriver   this may happen
il lui est arrivé un accident   he's had an accident
la neige lui arrivait (jusqu')aux genoux   the snow came
up to his knees

7 assaillir
to attack

PRESENT PARTICIPLE
assaillant

PAST PARTICIPLE
assailli

PRESENT		*IMPERFECT*	
j'	**assaille**	j'	**assaillais**
tu	**assailles**	tu	**assaillais**
il	**assaille**	il	**assaillait**
nous	**assaillons**	nous	**assaillions**
vous	**assaillez**	vous	**assailliez**
ils	**assaillent**	ils	**assaillaient**

		FUTURE	
		j'	**assaillirai**
		tu	**assailliras**
		il	**assaillira**
		nous	**assaillirons**
		vous	**assaillirez**
		ils	**assailliront**

IMPERATIVE		*CONDITIONAL*	
	assaille	j'	**assaillirais**
	assaillons	tu	**assaillirais**
	assaillez	il	**assaillirait**
		nous	**assaillirions**
		vous	**assailliriez**
		ils	**assailliraient**

PAST HISTORIC		PRESENT SUBJUNCTIVE	
j'	assaillis	j'	assaille
tu	assaillis	tu	assailles
il	assaillit	il	assaille
nous	assaillîmes	nous	assaillions
vous	assaillîtes	vous	assailliez
ils	assaillirent	ils	assaillent

PERFECT		PAST SUBJUNCTIVE	
j'	ai assailli	j'	assaillisse
tu	as assailli	tu	assaillisses
il	a assailli	il	assaillît
nous	avons assailli	nous	assaillissions
vous	avez assailli	vous	assaillissiez
ils	ont assailli	ils	assaillissent

CONSTRUCTIONS

on l'a assailli de questions he was bombarded with questions

27

8 s'asseoir
to sit down

PRESENT PARTICIPLE
s'asseyant

PAST PARTICIPLE
assis

PRESENT
je	**m'assieds**
tu	**t'assieds**
il	**s'assied**
nous	**nous asseyons**
vous	**vous asseyez**
ils	**s'asseyent**

ALTERNATIVE FORM OF
PRESENT
je	**m'assois**
tu	**t'assois**
il	**s'assoit**
nous	**nous assoyons**
vous	**vous assoyez**
ils	**s'assoient**

IMPERATIVE
assieds-toi
asseyons-nous
asseyez-vous

IMPERFECT
je	**m'asseyais**
tu	**t'asseyais**
il	**s'asseyait**
nous	**nous asseyions**
vous	**vous asseyiez**
ils	**s'asseyaient**

FUTURE
je	**m'assiérai**
tu	**t'assiéras**
il	**s'assiéra**
nous	**nous assiérons**
vous	**vous assiérez**
ils	**s'assiéront**

CONDITIONAL
je	**m'assiérais**
tu	**t'assiérais**
il	**s'assiérait**
nous	**nous assiérions**
vous	**vous assiériez**
ils	**s'assiéraient**

to sit down

PAST HISTORIC

je	m'assis
tu	t'assis
il	s'assit
nous	nous assîmes
vous	vous assîtes
ils	s'assirent

PRESENT SUBJUNCTIVE

je	m'asseye
tu	t'asseyes
il	s'asseye
nous	nous asseyions
vous	vous asseyiez
ils	s'asseyent

PERFECT

je	me suis assis
tu	t'es assis
il	s'est assis
nous	nous sommes assis
vous	vous êtes assis
ils	se sont assis

PAST SUBJUNCTIVE

je	m'assisse
tu	t'assisses
il	s'assît
nous	nous assissions
vous	vous assissiez
ils	s'assissent

CONSTRUCTIONS

veuillez vous asseoir please be seated
il s'est assis sur une chaise/par terre he sat (down) on a chair/the floor
il est assis sur une chaise/par terre he is sitting on a chair/the floor

9 attendre

to wait

PRESENT PARTICIPLE
attendant

PAST PARTICIPLE
attendu

PRESENT		*IMPERFECT*	
j'	**attends**	j'	**attendais**
tu	**attends**	tu	**attendais**
il	**attend**	il	**attendait**
nous	**attendons**	nous	**attendions**
vous	**attendez**	vous	**attendiez**
ils	**attendent**	ils	**attendaient**

		FUTURE	
		j'	**attendrai**
		tu	**attendras**
		il	**attendra**
		nous	**attendrons**
		vous	**attendrez**
		ils	**attendront**

IMPERATIVE	*CONDITIONAL*	
attends	j'	**attendrais**
attendons	tu	**attendrais**
attendez	il	**attendrait**
	nous	**attendrions**
	vous	**attendriez**
	ils	**attendraient**

PAST HISTORIC		PRESENT SUBJUNCTIVE	
j'	**attendis**	j'	**attende**
tu	**attendis**	tu	**attendes**
il	**attendit**	il	**attende**
nous	**attendîmes**	nous	**attendions**
vous	**attendîtes**	vous	**attendiez**
ils	**attendirent**	ils	**attendent**

PERFECT		PAST SUBJUNCTIVE	
j'	**ai attendu**	j'	**attendisse**
tu	**as attendu**	tu	**attendisses**
il	**a attendu**	il	**attendît**
nous	**avons attendu**	nous	**attendissions**
vous	**avez attendu**	vous	**attendissiez**
ils	**ont attendu**	ils	**attendissent**

CONSTRUCTIONS

nous attendons qu'il parte   we're waiting for him to leave
j'ai attendu 2 heures   I waited (for) 2 hours
attends d'être plus grand   wait till you're older
attendre qch de qn/qch   to expect sth of sb/sth
s'attendre à qch/à faire   to expect sth/to do

31

10 avoir
to have

PRESENT PARTICIPLE
ayant

PAST PARTICIPLE
eu

PRESENT		*IMPERFECT*	
j'	**ai**	j'	**avais**
tu	**as**	tu	**avais**
il	**a**	il	**avait**
nous	**avons**	nous	**avions**
vous	**avez**	vous	**aviez**
ils	**ont**	ils	**avaient**

		FUTURE	
		j'	**aurai**
		tu	**auras**
		il	**aura**
		nous	**aurons**
		vous	**aurez**
		ils	**auront**

IMPERATIVE	*CONDITIONAL*	
aie	j'	**aurais**
ayons	tu	**aurais**
ayez	il	**aurait**
	nous	**aurions**
	vous	**auriez**
	ils	**auraient**

PAST HISTORIC		PRESENT SUBJUNCTIVE	
j'	eus	j'	aie
tu	eus	tu	aies
il	eut	il	ait
nous	eûmes	nous	ayons
vous	eûtes	vous	ayez
ils	eurent	ils	aient

PERFECT		PAST SUBJUNCTIVE	
j'	ai eu	j'	eusse
tu	as eu	tu	eusses
il	a eu	il	eût
nous	avons eu	nous	eussions
vous	avez eu	vous	eussiez
ils	ont eu	ils	eussent

CONSTRUCTIONS

j'ai des lettres à écrire I've got letters to write
quel âge avez-vous? – j'ai 10 ans how old are you? – I'm 10 (years old)
avoir faim/chaud/tort to be hungry/hot/wrong
il y a there is; there are
il y la 10 ans 10 years ago

11 battre

to beat

PRESENT PARTICIPLE
battant

PAST PARTICIPLE
battu

also **abattre**
to pull down

combattre
to fight

débattre
to discuss

PRESENT		IMPERFECT	
je	**bats**	je	**batt**ais
tu	**bats**	tu	**batt**ais
il	**bat**	il	**batt**ait
nous	**batt**ons	nous	**batt**ions
vous	**batt**ez	vous	**batt**iez
ils	**batt**ent	ils	**batt**aient

FUTURE	
je	**batt**rai
tu	**batt**ras
il	**batt**ra
nous	**batt**rons
vous	**batt**rez
ils	**batt**ront

IMPERATIVE	CONDITIONAL	
bats	je	**batt**rais
battons	tu	**batt**rais
battez	il	**batt**rait
	nous	**batt**rions
	vous	**batt**riez
	ils	**batt**raient

rabattre
to pull down

PAST HISTORIC		*PRESENT SUBJUNCTIVE*	
je	**batt**is	je	**batt**e
tu	**batt**is	tu	**batt**es
il	**batt**it	il	**batt**e
nous	**batt**îmes	nous	**batt**ions
vous	**batt**îtes	vous	**batt**iez
ils	**batt**irent	ils	**batt**ent

PERFECT		*PAST SUBJUNCTIVE*	
j'	**ai batt**u	je	**batt**isse
tu	**as batt**u	tu	**batt**isses
il	**a batt**u	il	**batt**ît
nous	**avons batt**u	nous	**batt**issions
vous	**avez batt**u	vous	**batt**issiez
ils	**ont batt**u	ils	**batt**issent

CONSTRUCTIONS
battre des mains to clap one's hands
l'oiseau battait des ailes the bird was flapping its wings
se battre to fight

12 boire
to drink

PRESENT PARTICIPLE
buvant

PAST PARTICIPLE
bu

PRESENT		IMPERFECT	
je	bois	je	buvais
tu	bois	tu	buvais
il	boit	il	buvait
nous	buvons	nous	buvions
vous	buvez	vous	buviez
ils	boivent	ils	buvaient

		FUTURE	
		je	boirai
		tu	boiras
		il	boira
		nous	boirons
		vous	boirez
		ils	boiront

IMPERATIVE	CONDITIONAL	
bois	je	boirais
buvons	tu	boirais
buvez	il	boirait
	nous	boirions
	vous	boiriez
	ils	boiraient

PAST HISTORIC		PRESENT SUBJUNCTIVE	
je	**bus**	je	**boive**
tu	**bus**	tu	**boives**
il	**but**	il	**boive**
nous	**bûmes**	nous	**buvions**
vous	**bûtes**	vous	**buviez**
ils	**burent**	ils	**boivent**

PERFECT		PAST SUBJUNCTIVE	
j'	**ai** bu	je	**busse**
tu	**as** bu	tu	**busses**
il	**a** bu	il	**bût**
nous	**avons** bu	nous	**bussions**
vous	**avez** bu	vous	**bussiez**
ils	**ont** bu	ils	**bussent**

CONSTRUCTIONS
boire un verre   to have a drink

13 bouillir
to boil

PRESENT PARTICIPLE
bouillant

PAST PARTICIPLE
bouilli

PRESENT		*IMPERFECT*	
je	**bous**	je	**bouill**ais
tu	**bous**	tu	**bouill**ais
il	**bout**	il	**bouill**ait
nous	**bouill**ons	nous	**bouill**ions
vous	**bouill**ez	vous	**bouill**iez
ils	**bouill**ent	ils	**bouill**aient

		FUTURE	
		je	**bouill**irai
		tu	**bouill**iras
		il	**bouill**ira
		nous	**bouill**irons
		vous	**bouill**irez
		ils	**bouill**iront

IMPERATIVE		*CONDITIONAL*	
	bous	je	**bouill**irais
	bouillons	tu	**bouill**irais
	bouillez	il	**bouill**irait
		nous	**bouill**irions
		vous	**bouill**iriez
		ils	**bouill**iraient

PAST HISTORIC		PRESENT SUBJUNCTIVE	
je	bouillis	je	bouille
tu	bouillis	tu	bouilles
il	bouillit	il	bouille
nous	bouillîmes	nous	bouillions
vous	bouillîtes	vous	bouilliez
ils	bouillirent	ils	bouillent

PERFECT		PAST SUBJUNCTIVE	
j'	ai bouilli	je	bouillisse
tu	as bouilli	tu	bouillisses
il	a bouilli	il	bouillît
nous	avons bouilli	nous	bouillissions
vous	avez bouilli	vous	bouillissiez
ils	ont bouilli	ils	bouillissent

CONSTRUCTIONS

faire bouillir de l'eau/des pommes de terre to boil
water/potatoes

bouillir de colère/d'impatience to seethe with
anger/impatience

14 clore
to shut

PRESENT PARTICIPLE
closant

PAST PARTICIPLE
clos

PRESENT		*IMPERFECT*	
je	**clos**	je	**closais**
tu	**clos**	tu	**closais**
il	**clôt**	il	**closait**
nous	**closons**	nous	**closions**
vous	**closez**	vous	**closiez**
ils	**closent**	ils	**closaient**

		FUTURE	
		je	**clorai**
		tu	**cloras**
		il	**clora**
		nous	**clorons**
		vous	**clorez**
		ils	**cloront**

IMPERATIVE		*CONDITIONAL*	
	not used	je	**clorais**
		tu	**clorais**
		il	**clorait**
		nous	**clorions**
		vous	**cloriez**
		ils	**cloraient**

PAST HISTORIC	PRESENT SUBJUNCTIVE
not used	je **close**
	tu **closes**
	il **close**
	nous **closions**
	vous **closiez**
	ils **closent**
PERFECT	**PAST SUBJUNCTIVE**
j' **ai clos**	*not used*
tu **as clos**	
il **a clos**	
nous **avons clos**	
vous **avez clos**	
ils **ont clos**	

CONSTRUCTIONS

le débat s'est clos sur cette remarque the discussion ended with that remark

clore le bec à qn to shut sb up

15 commencer

to begin   *also* **annoncer**
       to announce

PRESENT PARTICIPLE
commençant

    avancer
       to move forward

PAST PARTICIPLE
commencé

    déplacer
       to move

PRESENT		IMPERFECT	
je	**commence**	je	**commençais**
tu	**commences**	tu	**commençais**
il	**commence**	il	**commençait**
nous	**commençons**	nous	**commencions**
vous	**commencez**	vous	**commenciez**
ils	**commencent**	ils	**commençaient**

		FUTURE	
		je	**commencerai**
		tu	**commenceras**
		il	**commencera**
		nous	**commencerons**
		vous	**commencerez**
		ils	**commenceront**

IMPERATIVE	CONDITIONAL	
commence	je	**commencerais**
commençons	tu	**commencerais**
commencez	il	**commencerait**
	nous	**commencerions**
	vous	**commenceriez**
	ils	**commenceraient**

effacer
   to erase

to begin

lancer
   to throw

PAST HISTORIC		PRESENT SUBJUNCTIVE	
je	**commençai**	je	**commence**
tu	**commenças**	tu	**commences**
il	**commença**	il	**commence**
nous	**commençâmes**	nous	**commencions**
vous	**commençâtes**	vous	**commenciez**
ils	**commencèrent**	ils	**commencent**

PERFECT		PAST SUBJUNCTIVE	
j'	**ai commencé**	je	**commençasse**
tu	**as commencé**	tu	**commençasses**
il	**a commencé**	il	**commençât**
nous	**avons commencé**	nous	**commençassions**
vous	**avez commencé**	vous	**commençassiez**
ils	**ont commencé**	ils	**commençassent**

CONSTRUCTIONS

commencer à *or* **de faire**   to begin to do
commencer par qch   to begin with sth
commencer par faire qch   to begin by doing sth
il commence à pleuvoir   it's beginning to rain

16 comprendre
to understand

PRESENT PARTICIPLE
comprenant

PAST PARTICIPLE
compris

PRESENT		IMPERFECT	
je	**comprend**s	je	comprenais
tu	**comprend**s	tu	comprenais
il	**comprend**	il	comprenait
nous	comprenons	nous	comprenions
vous	comprenez	vous	compreniez
ils	comprennent	ils	comprenaient

		FUTURE	
		je	**comprendr**ai
		tu	**comprendr**as
		il	**comprendr**a
		nous	**comprendr**ons
		vous	**comprendr**ez
		ils	**comprendr**ont

IMPERATIVE	CONDITIONAL	
comprends	je	**comprendr**ais
comprenons	tu	**comprendr**ais
comprenez	il	**comprendr**ait
	nous	**comprendr**ions
	vous	**comprendr**iez
	ils	**comprendr**aient

comprendre 16
to understand

<table>
<tr><td>

PAST HISTORIC
je	compris
tu	compris
il	comprit
nous	comprîmes
vous	comprîtes
ils	comprirent

</td><td>

PRESENT SUBJUNCTIVE
je	comprenne
tu	comprennes
il	comprenne
nous	comprenions
vous	compreniez
ils	comprennent

</td></tr>
<tr><td>

PERFECT
j'	ai	compris
tu	as	compris
il	a	compris
nous	avons	compris
vous	avez	compris
ils	ont	compris

</td><td>

PAST SUBJUNCTIVE
je	comprisse
tu	comprisses
il	comprît
nous	comprissions
vous	comprissiez
ils	comprissent

</td></tr>
</table>

CONSTRUCTIONS
la maison comprend 10 pièces   the house comprises 10 rooms
mal comprendre   to misunderstand
service compris   service charge included
100 F y compris l'électricité *or* **l'électricité y comprise**   100 F including electricity

17 conclure
to conclude   *also* **exclure**
                          to exclude

PRESENT PARTICIPLE
concluant

PAST PARTICIPLE
conclu

PRESENT		*IMPERFECT*	
je	**conclus**	je	**concluais**
tu	**conclus**	tu	**concluais**
il	**conclut**	il	**concluait**
nous	**concluons**	nous	**concluions**
vous	**concluez**	vous	**concluiez**
ils	**concluent**	ils	**concluaient**

		FUTURE	
		je	**conclurai**
		tu	**concluras**
		il	**conclura**
		nous	**conclurons**
		vous	**conclurez**
		ils	**concluront**

IMPERATIVE		*CONDITIONAL*	
	conclus	je	**conclurais**
	concluons	tu	**conclurais**
	concluez	il	**conclurait**
		nous	**conclurions**
		vous	**concluriez**
		ils	**concluraient**

conclure 17
to conclude

PAST HISTORIC	PRESENT SUBJUNCTIVE
je **conclus**	je **conclue**
tu **conclus**	tu **conclues**
il **conclut**	il **conclue**
nous **conclûmes**	nous **concluions**
vous **conclûtes**	vous **concluiez**
ils **conclurent**	ils **concluent**

PERFECT	PAST SUBJUNCTIVE
j' **ai conclu**	je **conclusse**
tu **as conclu**	tu **conclusses**
il **a conclu**	il **conclût**
nous **avons conclu**	nous **conclussions**
vous **avez conclu**	vous **conclussiez**
ils **ont conclu**	ils **conclussent**

CONSTRUCTIONS

marché conclu!   it's a deal!

j'en ai conclu qu'il était parti   I concluded that he had gone

ils ont conclu à son innocence   they concluded that he was innocent

18 conduire
to lead

also **éconduire**
to dismiss

PRESENT PARTICIPLE
conduisant

PAST PARTICIPLE
conduit

PRESENT

je	**conduis**
tu	**conduis**
il	**conduit**
nous	**conduisons**
vous	**conduisez**
ils	**conduisent**

IMPERFECT

je	**conduisais**
tu	**conduisais**
il	**conduisait**
nous	**conduisions**
vous	**conduisiez**
ils	**conduisaient**

FUTURE

je	**conduirai**
tu	**conduiras**
il	**conduira**
nous	**conduirons**
vous	**conduirez**
ils	**conduiront**

IMPERATIVE

conduis
conduisons
conduisez

CONDITIONAL

je	**conduirais**
tu	**conduirais**
il	**conduirait**
nous	**conduirions**
vous	**conduiriez**
ils	**conduiraient**

PRESENT PARTICIPLE
conduisant

PAST PARTICIPLE
conduit

PAST HISTORIC		PRESENT SUBJUNCTIVE	
je	**conduisis**	je	**conduise**
tu	**conduisis**	tu	**conduises**
il	**conduisit**	il	**conduise**
nous	**conduisîmes**	nous	**conduisions**
vous	**conduisîtes**	vous	**conduisiez**
ils	**conduisirent**	ils	**conduisent**

PERFECT		PAST SUBJUNCTIVE	
j'	**ai conduit**	je	**conduisisse**
tu	**as conduit**	tu	**conduisisses**
il	**a conduit**	il	**conduisît**
nous	**avons conduit**	nous	**conduisissions**
vous	**avez conduit**	vous	**conduisissiez**
ils	**ont conduit**	ils	**conduisissent**

CONSTRUCTIONS
conduire qn quelque part   to take sb somewhere; to drive sb somewhere
conduire qn à faire qch   to lead sb to do sth
cet escalier conduit au toit   these stairs lead (up) to the roof
se conduire   to behave (oneself)

19 connaître
to know

also **méconnaître**
to be unaware of

PRESENT PARTICIPLE
connaissant

reconnaître
to recognize

PAST PARTICIPLE
connu

PRESENT

je	**conn**ais
tu	**conn**ais
il	**conn**aît
nous	**conn**aissons
vous	**conn**aissez
ils	**conn**aissent

IMPERFECT

je	**conn**aissais
tu	**conn**aissais
il	**conn**aissait
nous	**conn**aissions
vous	**conn**aissiez
ils	**conn**aissaient

FUTURE

je	**conn**aîtrai
tu	**conn**aîtras
il	**conn**aîtra
nous	**conn**aîtrons
vous	**conn**aîtrez
ils	**conn**aîtront

IMPERATIVE

connais
connaissons
connaissez

CONDITIONAL

je	**conn**aîtrais
tu	**conn**aîtrais
il	**conn**aîtrait
nous	**conn**aîtrions
vous	**conn**aîtriez
ils	**conn**aîtraient

PAST HISTORIC		PRESENT SUBJUNCTIVE	
je	connus	je	connaisse
tu	connus	tu	connaisses
il	connut	il	connaisse
nous	connûmes	nous	connaissions
vous	connûtes	vous	connaissiez
ils	connurent	ils	connaissent

PERFECT		PAST SUBJUNCTIVE	
j'	ai connu	je	connusse
tu	as connu	tu	connusses
il	a connu	il	connût
nous	avons connu	nous	connussions
vous	avez connu	vous	connussiez
ils	ont connu	ils	connussent

CONSTRUCTIONS

connaître qn de vue/nom to know sb by sight/name
il connaît bien la littérature anglaise he's very familiar
with English literature
faire connaître qn à qn to introduce sb to sb
se faire connaître to make a name for oneself; to
introduce oneself

20 coudre
to sew

PRESENT PARTICIPLE
cousant

PAST PARTICIPLE
cousu

PRESENT		IMPERFECT	
je	**coud**s	je	cousais
tu	**coud**s	tu	cousais
il	**coud**	il	cousait
nous	cousons	nous	cousions
vous	cousez	vous	cousiez
ils	cousent	ils	cousaient

		FUTURE	
		je	**coudr**ai
		tu	**coudr**as
		il	**coudr**a
		nous	**coudr**ons
		vous	**coudr**ez
		ils	**coudr**ont

IMPERATIVE	CONDITIONAL	
couds	je	**coudr**ais
cousons	tu	**coudr**ais
cousez	il	**coudr**ait
	nous	**coudr**ions
	vous	**coudr**iez
	ils	**coudr**aient

PAST HISTORIC		PRESENT SUBJUNCTIVE	
je	cousis	je	couse
tu	cousis	tu	couses
il	cousit	il	couse
nous	cousîmes	nous	cousions
vous	cousîtes	vous	cousiez
ils	cousirent	ils	cousent

PERFECT		PAST SUBJUNCTIVE	
j'	**ai** cousu	je	cousisse
tu	**as** cousu	tu	cousisses
il	**a** cousu	il	cousît
nous	**avons** cousu	nous	cousissions
vous	**avez** cousu	vous	cousissiez
ils	**ont** cousu	ils	cousissent

CONSTRUCTIONS
coudre un bouton à une veste to sew a button on a
jacket

21 courir

to run

also **accourir**
to rush

PRESENT PARTICIPLE
courant

concourir
to compete

PAST PARTICIPLE
couru

parcourir
to go through

PRESENT		*IMPERFECT*	
je	**cours**	je	**cour**ais
tu	**cours**	tu	**cour**ais
il	**court**	il	**cour**ait
nous	**cour**ons	nous	**cour**ions
vous	**cour**ez	vous	**cour**iez
ils	**cour**ent	ils	**cour**aient

		FUTURE	
		je	**cour**rai
		tu	**cour**ras
		il	**cour**ra
		nous	**cour**rons
		vous	**cour**rez
		ils	**cour**ront

IMPERATIVE		*CONDITIONAL*	
	cours	je	**cour**rais
	courons	tu	**cour**rais
	courez	il	**cour**rait
		nous	**cour**rions
		vous	**cour**riez
		ils	**cour**raient

secourir
to rescue

PAST HISTORIC		PRESENT SUBJUNCTIVE	
je	**cour**us	je	**cour**e
tu	**cour**us	tu	**cour**es
il	**cour**ut	il	**cour**e
nous	**cour**ûmes	nous	**cour**ions
vous	**cour**ûtes	vous	**cour**iez
ils	**cour**urent	ils	**cour**ent

PERFECT		PAST SUBJUNCTIVE	
j'	**ai cour**u	je	**cour**usse
tu	**as cour**u	tu	**cour**usses
il	**a cour**u	il	**cour**ût
nous	**avons cour**u	nous	**cour**ussions
vous	**avez cour**u	vous	**cour**ussiez
ils	**ont cour**u	ils	**cour**ussent

CONSTRUCTIONS
courir faire qch   to rush and do sth
courir à toutes jambes   to run as fast as one's legs can carry one
le bruit court que ...   the rumour is going round that ...
courir le risque de   to run the risk of

22 couvrir

to cover

also **recouvrir**
to re-cover

PRESENT PARTICIPLE
couvrant

PAST PARTICIPLE
couvert

PRESENT		IMPERFECT	
je	**couvre**	je	**couvrais**
tu	**couvres**	tu	**couvrais**
il	**couvre**	il	**couvrait**
nous	**couvrons**	nous	**couvrions**
vous	**couvrez**	vous	**couvriez**
ils	**couvrent**	ils	**couvraient**

		FUTURE	
		je	**couvrirai**
		tu	**couvriras**
		il	**couvrira**
		nous	**couvrirons**
		vous	**couvrirez**
		ils	**couvriront**

IMPERATIVE	CONDITIONAL	
couvre	je	**couvrirais**
couvrons	tu	**couvrirais**
couvrez	il	**couvrirait**
	nous	**couvririons**
	vous	**couvririez**
	ils	**couvriraient**

PAST HISTORIC
- je **couvris**
- tu **couvris**
- il **couvrit**
- nous **couvrîmes**
- vous **couvrîtes**
- ils **couvrirent**

PRESENT SUBJUNCTIVE
- je **couvre**
- tu **couvres**
- il **couvre**
- nous **couvrions**
- vous **couvriez**
- ils **couvrent**

PERFECT
- j' **ai couvert**
- tu **as couvert**
- il **a couvert**
- nous **avons couvert**
- vous **avez couvert**
- ils **ont couvert**

PAST SUBJUNCTIVE
- je **couvrisse**
- tu **couvrisses**
- il **couvrît**
- nous **couvrissions**
- vous **couvrissiez**
- ils **couvrissent**

CONSTRUCTIONS

la voiture nous a couverts de boue the car covered us in mud

couvrir qn de cadeaux to shower sb with gifts

elle s'est couvert le visage des mains she covered her face with her hands

couvrez-vous bien! wrap up well!

23 craindre

to fear

also **contraindre**
to compel

PRESENT PARTICIPLE
craignant

plaindre
to pity

PAST PARTICIPLE
craint

PRESENT		IMPERFECT	
je	**crains**	je	**craignais**
tu	**crains**	tu	**craignais**
il	**craint**	il	**craignait**
nous	**craignons**	nous	**craignions**
vous	**craignez**	vous	**craigniez**
ils	**craignent**	ils	**craignaient**

		FUTURE	
		je	**craindrai**
		tu	**craindras**
		il	**craindra**
		nous	**craindrons**
		vous	**craindrez**
		ils	**craindront**

IMPERATIVE	CONDITIONAL	
crains	je	**craindrais**
craignons	tu	**craindrais**
craignez	il	**craindrait**
	nous	**craindrions**
	vous	**craindriez**
	ils	**craindraient**

PAST HISTORIC		PRESENT SUBJUNCTIVE	
je	craignis	je	craigne
tu	craignis	tu	craignes
il	craignit	il	craigne
nous	craignîmes	nous	craignions
vous	craignîtes	vous	craigniez
ils	craignirent	ils	craignent

PERFECT		PAST SUBJUNCTIVE	
j'	ai craint	je	craignisse
tu	as craint	tu	craignisses
il	a craint	il	craignît
nous	avons craint	nous	craignissions
vous	avez craint	vous	craignissiez
ils	ont craint	ils	craignissent

CONSTRUCTIONS

ne craignez rien don't be afraid
craindre de faire qch to be afraid of doing sth
ces plantes craignent la chaleur these plants dislike heat

24 créer

to create   *also* **agréer**
to accept

PRESENT PARTICIPLE
créant

               maugréer
to grumble

PAST PARTICIPLE
créé

               procréer
to procreate

PRESENT		IMPERFECT	
je	**crée**	je	**créais**
tu	**crées**	tu	**créais**
il	**crée**	il	**créait**
nous	**créons**	nous	**créions**
vous	**créez**	vous	**créiez**
ils	**créent**	ils	**créaient**

		FUTURE	
		je	**créerai**
		tu	**créeras**
		il	**créera**
		nous	**créerons**
		vous	**créerez**
		ils	**créeront**

IMPERATIVE	CONDITIONAL	
crée	je	**créerais**
créons	tu	**créerais**
créez	il	**créerait**
	nous	**créerions**
	vous	**créeriez**
	ils	**créeraient**

PAST HISTORIC		PRESENT SUBJUNCTIVE	
je	**créai**	je	**crée**
tu	**créas**	tu	**crées**
il	**créa**	il	**crée**
nous	**créâmes**	nous	**créions**
vous	**créâtes**	vous	**créiez**
ils	**créèrent**	ils	**créent**

PERFECT		PAST SUBJUNCTIVE	
j'	**ai créé**	je	**créasse**
tu	**as créé**	tu	**créasses**
il	**a créé**	il	**créât**
nous	**avons créé**	nous	**créassions**
vous	**avez créé**	vous	**créassiez**
ils	**ont créé**	ils	**créassent**

CONSTRUCTIONS

il nous a créé des ennuis   he's caused us problems
il s'est créé une clientèle   he has built up custom

25 crier

to shout

also **amplifier**
to amplify

PRESENT PARTICIPLE
criant

associer
to associate

PAST PARTICIPLE
crié

copier
to copy

PRESENT

je	**crie**
tu	**cries**
il	**crie**
nous	**crions**
vous	**criez**
ils	**crient**

IMPERFECT

je	**criais**
tu	**criais**
il	**criait**
nous	**criions**
vous	**criiez**
ils	**criaient**

FUTURE

je	**crierai**
tu	**crieras**
il	**criera**
nous	**crierons**
vous	**crierez**
ils	**crieront**

IMPERATIVE

crie
crions
criez

CONDITIONAL

je	**crierais**
tu	**crierais**
il	**crierait**
nous	**crierions**
vous	**crieriez**
ils	**crieraient**

to shout

étudier
  to study

marier
  to marry

PAST HISTORIC		PRESENT SUBJUNCTIVE	
je	criai	je	crie
tu	crias	tu	cries
il	cria	il	crie
nous	criâmes	nous	criions
vous	criâtes	vous	criiez
ils	crièrent	ils	crient

PERFECT		PAST SUBJUNCTIVE	
j'	ai crié	je	criasse
tu	as crié	tu	criasses
il	a crié	il	criât
nous	avons crié	nous	criassions
vous	avez crié	vous	criassiez
ils	ont crié	ils	criassent

CONSTRUCTIONS

crier à tue-tête to shout one's head off
crier contre or **après qn** to nag (at) sb
crier à qn de faire qch to shout at sb to do sth
crier qch sur les toits to proclaim sth from the rooftops
crier au secours to shout for help

26 croire
to believe

PRESENT PARTICIPLE
croyant

PAST PARTICIPLE
cru

PRESENT		*IMPERFECT*	
je	**crois**	je	**croyais**
tu	**crois**	tu	**croyais**
il	**croit**	il	**croyait**
nous	**croyons**	nous	**croyions**
vous	**croyez**	vous	**croyiez**
ils	**croient**	ils	**croyaient**

		FUTURE	
		je	**croirai**
		tu	**croiras**
		il	**croira**
		nous	**croirons**
		vous	**croirez**
		ils	**croiront**

IMPERATIVE		*CONDITIONAL*	
	crois	je	**croirais**
	croyons	tu	**croirais**
	croyez	il	**croirait**
		nous	**croirions**
		vous	**croiriez**
		ils	**croiraient**

croire 26
to believe

PAST HISTORIC		PRESENT SUBJUNCTIVE	
je	crus	je	croie
tu	crus	tu	croies
il	crut	il	croie
nous	crûmes	nous	croyions
vous	crûtes	vous	croyiez
ils	crurent	ils	croient

PERFECT		PAST SUBJUNCTIVE	
j'	ai cru	je	crusse
tu	as cru	tu	crusses
il	a cru	il	crût
nous	avons cru	nous	crussions
vous	avez cru	vous	crussiez
ils	ont cru	ils	crussent

CONSTRUCTIONS

croire aux fantômes/en Dieu to believe in ghosts/God
on l'a cru mort he was presumed (to be) dead
elle croyait avoir perdu son sac she thought she had lost her bag
je crois que oui I think so, I think we will *etc*

27 croître

to grow

PRESENT PARTICIPLE
croissant

PAST PARTICIPLE
crû (*NB*: **crue, crus, crues**)

	PRESENT		*IMPERFECT*
je	**croîs**	je	**croissais**
tu	**croîs**	tu	**croissais**
il	**croît**	il	**croissait**
nous	**croissons**	nous	**croissions**
vous	**croissez**	vous	**croissiez**
ils	**croissent**	ils	**croissaient**

			FUTURE
		je	**croîtrai**
		tu	**croîtras**
		il	**croîtra**
		nous	**croîtrons**
		vous	**croîtrez**
		ils	**croîtront**

IMPERATIVE			*CONDITIONAL*
	croîs	je	**croîtrais**
	croissons	tu	**croîtrais**
	croissez	il	**croîtrait**
		nous	**croîtrions**
		vous	**croîtriez**
		ils	**croîtraient**

66

PAST HISTORIC		PRESENT SUBJUNCTIVE	
je	crûs	je	croisse
tu	crûs	tu	croisses
il	crût	il	croisse
nous	crûmes	nous	croissions
vous	crûtes	vous	croissiez
ils	crûrent	ils	croissent

PERFECT		PAST SUBJUNCTIVE	
j'	ai crû	je	crûsse
tu	as crû	tu	crûsses
il	a crû	il	crût
nous	avons crû	nous	crûssions
vous	avez crû	vous	crûssiez
ils	ont crû	ils	crûssent

CONSTRUCTIONS

croître en beauté/nombre   to grow in beauty/number
les jours croissent   the days are getting longer

28 cueillir

to pick

also accueillir
to welcome

recueillir
to collect

PRESENT PARTICIPLE
cueillant

PAST PARTICIPLE
cueilli

PRESENT

je	**cueille**
tu	**cueilles**
il	**cueille**
nous	**cueillons**
vous	**cueillez**
ils	**cueillent**

IMPERFECT

je	**cueillais**
tu	**cueillais**
il	**cueillait**
nous	**cueillions**
vous	**cueilliez**
ils	**cueillaient**

FUTURE

je	**cueillerai**
tu	**cueilleras**
il	**cueillera**
nous	**cueillerons**
vous	**cueillerez**
ils	**cueilleront**

IMPERATIVE

cueille
cueillons
cueillez

CONDITIONAL

je	**cueillerais**
tu	**cueillerais**
il	**cueillerait**
nous	**cueillerions**
vous	**cueilleriez**
ils	**cueilleraient**

PAST HISTORIC		PRESENT SUBJUNCTIVE	
je	cueillis	je	cueille
tu	cueillis	tu	cueilles
il	cueillit	il	cueille
nous	cueillîmes	nous	cueillions
vous	cueillîtes	vous	cueilliez
ils	cueillirent	ils	cueillent

PERFECT		PAST SUBJUNCTIVE	
j'	ai cueilli	je	cueillisse
tu	as cueilli	tu	cueillisses
il	a cueilli	il	cueillît
nous	avons cueilli	nous	cueillissions
vous	avez cueilli	vous	cueillissiez
ils	ont cueilli	ils	cueillissent

CONSTRUCTIONS

cueillir qn à froid to catch sb off guard

29 cuire

to cook

also **construire**
to build

PRESENT PARTICIPLE
cuisant

instruire
to teach

PAST PARTICIPLE
cuit

produire
to produce

PRESENT		*IMPERFECT*	
je	**cuis**	je	**cuisais**
tu	**cuis**	tu	**cuisais**
il	**cuit**	il	**cuisait**
nous	**cuisons**	nous	**cuisions**
vous	**cuisez**	vous	**cuisiez**
ils	**cuisent**	ils	**cuisaient**

		FUTURE	
		je	**cuirai**
		tu	**cuiras**
		il	**cuira**
		nous	**cuirons**
		vous	**cuirez**
		ils	**cuiront**

IMPERATIVE		*CONDITIONAL*	
	cuis	je	**cuirais**
	cuisons	tu	**cuirais**
	cuisez	il	**cuirait**
		nous	**cuirions**
		vous	**cuiriez**
		ils	**cuiraient**

réduire
　to reduce

séduire
　to charm

PAST HISTORIC		PRESENT SUBJUNCTIVE	
je	**cuis**is	je	**cuis**e
tu	**cuis**is	tu	**cuis**es
il	**cuis**it	il	**cuis**e
nous	**cuis**îmes	nous	**cuis**ions
vous	**cuis**îtes	vous	**cuis**iez
ils	**cuis**irent	ils	**cuis**ent

PERFECT		PAST SUBJUNCTIVE	
j'	**ai cuit**	je	**cuis**isse
tu	**as cuit**	tu	**cuis**isses
il	**a cuit**	il	**cuis**ît
nous	**avons cuit**	nous	**cuis**issions
vous	**avez cuit**	vous	**cuis**issiez
ils	**ont cuit**	ils	**cuis**issent

CONSTRUCTIONS

cuire au gaz/à l'électricité　to cook with gas/by electricity
cuire au four　to bake; to roast
cuire à la vapeur　to steam
cuire à feu doux　to cook gently
bien cuit　well done

30 découvrir
to discover

PRESENT PARTICIPLE
découvrant

PAST PARTICIPLE
découvert

PRESENT		*IMPERFECT*	
je	**découvre**	je	**découvrais**
tu	**découvres**	tu	**découvrais**
il	**découvre**	il	**découvrait**
nous	**découvrons**	nous	**découvrions**
vous	**découvrez**	vous	**découvriez**
ils	**découvrent**	ils	**découvraient**

		FUTURE	
		je	**découvrirai**
		tu	**découvriras**
		il	**découvrira**
		nous	**découvrirons**
		vous	**découvrirez**
		ils	**découvriront**

IMPERATIVE		*CONDITIONAL*	
	découvre	je	**découvrirais**
	découvrons	tu	**découvrirais**
	découvrez	il	**découvrirait**
		nous	**découvririons**
		vous	**découvririez**
		ils	**découvriraient**

PAST HISTORIC		PRESENT SUBJUNCTIVE	
je	**découvri**s	je	**découvre**
tu	**découvri**s	tu	**découvres**
il	**découvri**t	il	**découvre**
nous	**découvrî**mes	nous	**découvrions**
vous	**découvrî**tes	vous	**découvriez**
ils	**découvri**rent	ils	**découvrent**

PERFECT		PAST SUBJUNCTIVE	
j'	**ai** découvert	je	**découvrisse**
tu	**as** découvert	tu	**découvrisses**
il	**a** découvert	il	**découvrît**
nous	**avons** découvert	nous	**découvrissions**
vous	**avez** découvert	vous	**découvrissiez**
ils	**ont** découvert	ils	**découvrissent**

CONSTRUCTIONS

il craint d'être découvert he's afraid of being found out
une robe qui découvre les épaules a dress which reveals the shoulders
se découvrir to take off one's hat; to undress

31 descendre
to go down

PRESENT PARTICIPLE
descendant

PAST PARTICIPLE
descendu

PRESENT		*IMPERFECT*	
je	**descend**s	je	**descend**ais
tu	**descend**s	tu	**descend**ais
il	**descend**	il	**descend**ait
nous	**descend**ons	nous	**descend**ions
vous	**descend**ez	vous	**descend**iez
ils	**descend**ent	ils	**descend**aient

		FUTURE	
		je	**descend**rai
		tu	**descend**ras
		il	**descend**ra
		nous	**descend**rons
		vous	**descend**rez
		ils	**descend**ront

IMPERATIVE	*CONDITIONAL*	
descends	je	**descend**rais
descendons	tu	**descend**rais
descendez	il	**descend**rait
	nous	**descend**rions
	vous	**descend**riez
	ils	**descend**raient

to go down

PAST HISTORIC		PRESENT SUBJUNCTIVE	
je	**descendis**	je	**descende**
tu	**descendis**	tu	**descendes**
il	**descendit**	il	**descende**
nous	**descendîmes**	nous	**descendions**
vous	**descendîtes**	vous	**descendiez**
ils	**descendirent**	ils	**descendent**

PERFECT		PAST SUBJUNCTIVE	
je	**suis descendu**	je	**descendisse**
tu	**es descendu**	tu	**descendisses**
il	**est descendu**	il	**descendît**
nous	**sommes descendus**	nous	**descendissions**
vous	**êtes descendu(s)**	vous	**descendissiez**
ils	**sont descendus**	ils	**descendissent**

CONSTRUCTIONS

descendre de voiture/du train/de bicyclette to get out of the car/off the train/off one's bicycle
sa jupe lui descend jusqu'aux chevilles her skirt comes down to her ankles
il a descendu la valise he took the case down

32 détruire
to destroy

PRESENT PARTICIPLE
détruisant

PAST PARTICIPLE
détruit

PRESENT		*IMPERFECT*	
je	**détruis**	je	**détrui**sais
tu	**détruis**	tu	**détrui**sais
il	**détruit**	il	**détrui**sait
nous	**détruis**ons	nous	**détrui**sions
vous	**détruis**ez	vous	**détrui**siez
ils	**détruis**ent	ils	**détrui**saient

		FUTURE	
		je	**détrui**rai
		tu	**détrui**ras
		il	**détrui**ra
		nous	**détrui**rons
		vous	**détrui**rez
		ils	**détrui**ront

IMPERATIVE		*CONDITIONAL*	
	détruis	je	**détrui**rais
	détruisons	tu	**détrui**rais
	détruisez	il	**détrui**rait
		nous	**détrui**rions
		vous	**détrui**riez
		ils	**détrui**raient

PAST HISTORIC		PRESENT SUBJUNCTIVE	
je	**détrui**sis	je	**détrui**se
tu	**détrui**sis	tu	**détrui**ses
il	**détrui**sit	il	**détrui**se
nous	**détrui**sîmes	nous	**détrui**sions
vous	**détrui**sîtes	vous	**détrui**siez
ils	**détrui**sirent	ils	**détrui**sent

PERFECT		PAST SUBJUNCTIVE	
j'	**ai détrui**t	je	**détrui**sisse
tu	**as détrui**t	tu	**détrui**sisses
il	**a détrui**t	il	**détrui**sît
nous	**avons détrui**t	nous	**détrui**sissions
vous	**avez détrui**t	vous	**détrui**sissiez
ils	**ont détrui**t	ils	**détrui**sissent

CONSTRUCTIONS
détruire par le feu   to destroy by fire

33 devenir
to become

PRESENT PARTICIPLE
devenant

PAST PARTICIPLE
devenu

PRESENT		*IMPERFECT*	
je	**deviens**	je	**deven**ais
tu	**deviens**	tu	**deven**ais
il	**devient**	il	**deven**ait
nous	**deven**ons	nous	**deven**ions
vous	**deven**ez	vous	**deven**iez
ils	**deviennent**	ils	**deven**aient

		FUTURE	
		je	**deviendr**ai
		tu	**deviendr**as
		il	**deviendr**a
		nous	**deviendr**ons
		vous	**deviendr**ez
		ils	**deviendr**ont

IMPERATIVE		*CONDITIONAL*	
	deviens	je	**deviendr**ais
	devenons	tu	**deviendr**ais
	devenez	il	**deviendr**ait
		nous	**deviendr**ions
		vous	**deviendr**iez
		ils	**deviendr**aient

PAST HISTORIC		PRESENT SUBJUNCTIVE	
je	devins	je	devienne
tu	devins	tu	deviennes
il	devint	il	devienne
nous	devînmes	nous	**deven**ions
vous	devîntes	vous	**deven**iez
ils	devinrent	ils	deviennent

PERFECT		PAST SUBJUNCTIVE	
je	suis **deven**u	je	devinsse
tu	es **deven**u	tu	devinsses
il	est **deven**u	il	devînt
nous	sommes **deven**us	nous	devinssions
vous	êtes **deven**u(s)	vous	devinssiez
ils	sont **deven**us	ils	devinssent

CONSTRUCTIONS

devenir médecin/professeur   to become a doctor/a teacher

devenir vieux/grand   to get old/tall

qu'est-il devenu?   what has become of him?

il devient de plus en plus agressif   he's growing increasingly aggressive

34 devoir

to have to; to owe

PRESENT PARTICIPLE
devant

PAST PARTICIPLE
dû (*NB*: **due, dus, dues**)

PRESENT		IMPERFECT	
je	**dois**	je	**dev**ais
tu	**dois**	tu	**dev**ais
il	**doit**	il	**dev**ait
nous	**devons**	nous	**dev**ions
vous	**devez**	vous	**dev**iez
ils	**doivent**	ils	**dev**aient

		FUTURE	
		je	**dev**rai
		tu	**dev**ras
		il	**dev**ra
		nous	**dev**rons
		vous	**dev**rez
		ils	**dev**ront

IMPERATIVE	CONDITIONAL	
dois	je	**dev**rais
devons	tu	**dev**rais
devez	il	**dev**rait
	nous	**dev**rions
	vous	**dev**riez
	ils	**dev**raient

PAST HISTORIC		PRESENT SUBJUNCTIVE	
je	dus	je	doive
tu	dus	tu	doives
il	dut	il	doive
nous	dûmes	nous	**dev**ions
vous	dûtes	vous	**dev**iez
ils	dûrent	ils	doivent

PERFECT		PAST SUBJUNCTIVE	
j'	**ai** dû	je	dusse
tu	**as** dû	tu	dusses
il	**a** dû	il	dût
nous	**avons** dû	nous	dussions
vous	**avez** dû	vous	dussiez
ils	**ont** dû	ils	dussent

CONSTRUCTIONS
devoir qch à qn to owe sb sth
devoir faire qch to have to do sth
il doit arriver ce soir he is due (to arrive) tonight
il a dû s'égarer he must have got lost
ceci est dû à … this is due to …

35 dire
to say

PRESENT PARTICIPLE
disant

PAST PARTICIPLE
dit

PRESENT		IMPERFECT	
je	dis	je	disais
tu	dis	tu	disais
il	dit	il	disait
nous	disons	nous	disions
vous	dites	vous	disiez
ils	disent	ils	disaient

		FUTURE	
		je	dirai
		tu	diras
		il	dira
		nous	dirons
		vous	direz
		ils	diront

IMPERATIVE	CONDITIONAL	
dis	je	dirais
disons	tu	dirais
dites	il	dirait
	nous	dirions
	vous	diriez
	ils	diraient

to say

PAST HISTORIC		PRESENT SUBJUNCTIVE	
je	dis	je	dise
tu	dis	tu	dises
il	dit	il	dise
nous	dîmes	nous	disions
vous	dîtes	vous	disiez
ils	dirent	ils	disent

PERFECT		PAST SUBJUNCTIVE	
j'	ai dit	je	disse
tu	as dit	tu	disses
il	a dit	il	dît
nous	avons dit	nous	dissions
vous	avez dit	vous	dissiez
ils	ont dit	ils	dissent

CONSTRUCTIONS

dire qch à qn to tell sb sth
dire à qn de faire qch to tell sb to do sth
cela ne me dit rien I don't fancy it
on dirait du poulet it tastes like chicken
on dirait Jean it looks like John

36 donner
to give

also **accepter**
to accept

PRESENT PARTICIPLE
donnant

causer
to cause

PAST PARTICIPLE
donné

laver
to wash

PRESENT

je	**donne**
tu	**donnes**
il	**donne**
nous	**donnons**
vous	**donnez**
ils	**donnent**

IMPERFECT

je	**donnais**
tu	**donnais**
il	**donnait**
nous	**donnions**
vous	**donniez**
ils	**donnaient**

FUTURE

je	**donnerai**
tu	**donneras**
il	**donnera**
nous	**donnerons**
vous	**donnerez**
ils	**donneront**

IMPERATIVE

donne
donnons
donnez

CONDITIONAL

je	**donnerais**
tu	**donnerais**
il	**donnerait**
nous	**donnerions**
vous	**donneriez**
ils	**donneraient**

poser
to put

rêver
to dream

to give

PAST HISTORIC
je	**donn**ai
tu	**donn**as
il	**donn**a
nous	**donn**âmes
vous	**donn**âtes
ils	**donn**èrent

PRESENT SUBJUNCTIVE
je	**donn**e
tu	**donn**es
il	**donn**e
nous	**donn**ions
vous	**donn**iez
ils	**donn**ent

PERFECT
j'	**ai donné**
tu	**as donné**
il	**a donné**
nous	**avons donné**
vous	**avez donné**
ils	**ont donné**

PAST SUBJUNCTIVE
je	**donn**asse
tu	**donn**asses
il	**donn**ât
nous	**donn**assions
vous	**donn**assiez
ils	**donn**assent

CONSTRUCTIONS

donner qch à qn   to give sb sth
donner quelque chose à faire à qn   to give sb something to do
donner à boire à qn   to give sb something to drink
cela me donne soif   this makes me (feel) thirsty
donner sur   to open onto; to overlook

37 dormir
to sleep

also s'endormir
to fall asleep

PRESENT PARTICIPLE
dormant

PAST PARTICIPLE
dormi

PRESENT		*IMPERFECT*	
je	**dors**	je	**dormais**
tu	**dors**	tu	**dormais**
il	**dort**	il	**dormait**
nous	**dormons**	nous	**dormions**
vous	**dormez**	vous	**dormiez**
ils	**dorment**	ils	**dormaient**

		FUTURE	
		je	**dormirai**
		tu	**dormiras**
		il	**dormira**
		nous	**dormirons**
		vous	**dormirez**
		ils	**dormiront**

IMPERATIVE	*CONDITIONAL*	
dors	je	**dormirais**
dormons	tu	**dormirais**
dormez	il	**dormirait**
	nous	**dormirions**
	vous	**dormiriez**
	ils	**dormiraient**

PAST HISTORIC		PRESENT SUBJUNCTIVE	
je	**dorm**is	je	**dorm**e
tu	**dorm**is	tu	**dorm**es
il	**dorm**it	il	**dorm**e
nous	**dorm**îmes	nous	**dorm**ions
vous	**dorm**îtes	vous	**dorm**iez
ils	**dorm**irent	ils	**dorm**ent

PERFECT		PAST SUBJUNCTIVE	
j'	**ai dormi**	je	**dorm**isse
tu	**as dormi**	tu	**dorm**isses
il	**a dormi**	il	**dorm**ît
nous	**avons dormi**	nous	**dorm**issions
vous	**avez dormi**	vous	**dorm**issiez
ils	**ont dormi**	ils	**dorm**issent

CONSTRUCTIONS

il dort he's asleep

j'ai mal dormi I didn't sleep well

il dort d'un sommeil léger he's a light sleeper

je n'ai pas dormi de la nuit I didn't sleep a wink (all night)

38 écrire

to write

also décrire

to describe

PRESENT PARTICIPLE
écrivant

inscrire
to write

PAST PARTICIPLE
écrit

souscrire
to subscribe

PRESENT		*IMPERFECT*	
j'	écris	j'	écrivais
tu	écris	tu	écrivais
il	écrit	il	écrivait
nous	écrivons	nous	écrivions
vous	écrivez	vous	écriviez
ils	écrivent	ils	écrivaient

		FUTURE	
		j'	écrirai
		tu	écriras
		il	écrira
		nous	écrirons
		vous	écrirez
		ils	écriront

IMPERATIVE		*CONDITIONAL*	
	écris	j'	écrirais
	écrivons	tu	écrirais
	écrivez	il	écrirait
		nous	écririons
		vous	écririez
		ils	écriraient

transcrire
to transcribe

PAST HISTORIC		*PRESENT SUBJUNCTIVE*	
j'	**écriv**is	j'	**écrive**
tu	**écriv**is	tu	**écrives**
il	**écriv**it	il	**écrive**
nous	**écriv**îmes	nous	**écrivions**
vous	**écriv**îtes	vous	**écriviez**
ils	**écriv**irent	ils	**écrivent**

PERFECT		*PAST SUBJUNCTIVE*	
j'	**ai écrit**	j'	**écrivisse**
tu	**as écrit**	tu	**écrivisses**
il	**a écrit**	il	**écrivît**
nous	**avons écrit**	nous	**écrivissions**
vous	**avez écrit**	vous	**écrivissiez**
ils	**ont écrit**	ils	**écrivissent**

CONSTRUCTIONS
écrit à la main / à la machine   handwritten / typed
appeler s'écrit avec deux p   appeler is spelt with two ps

39 entrer
to enter

PRESENT PARTICIPLE
entrant

PAST PARTICIPLE
entré

PRESENT
j'	**entre**
tu	**entres**
il	**entre**
nous	**entrons**
vous	**entrez**
ils	**entrent**

IMPERATIVE
entre
entrons
entrez

IMPERFECT
j'	**entrais**
tu	**entrais**
il	**entrait**
nous	**entrions**
vous	**entriez**
ils	**entraient**

FUTURE
j'	**entrerai**
tu	**entreras**
il	**entrera**
nous	**entrerons**
vous	**entrerez**
ils	**entreront**

CONDITIONAL
j'	**entrerais**
tu	**entrerais**
il	**entrerait**
nous	**entrerions**
vous	**entreriez**
ils	**entreraient**

PAST HISTORIC		PRESENT SUBJUNCTIVE	
j'	**entrai**	j'	**entre**
tu	**entras**	tu	**entres**
il	**entra**	il	**entre**
nous	**entrâmes**	nous	**entrions**
vous	**entrâtes**	vous	**entriez**
ils	**entrèrent**	ils	**entrent**

PERFECT		PAST SUBJUNCTIVE	
je	**suis entré**	j'	**entrasse**
tu	**es entré**	tu	**entrasses**
il	**est entré**	il	**entrât**
nous	**sommes entrés**	nous	**entrassions**
vous	**êtes entré(s)**	vous	**entrassiez**
ils	**sont entrés**	ils	**entrassent**

CONSTRUCTIONS

entrer dans une pièce/une voiture to go (*or* come) into a room/get into a car
faire entrer qn to show *or* ask sb in
entrer dans un club/une firme to join a club/firm
ça n'entre pas dans ce tiroir it won't go into this drawer

40 envoyer

to send

also renvoyer
to send back

PRESENT PARTICIPLE
envoyant

PAST PARTICIPLE
envoyé

PRESENT		IMPERFECT	
j'	**envoi**e	j'	**envoy**ais
tu	**envoi**es	tu	**envoy**ais
il	**envoi**e	il	**envoy**ait
nous	**envoy**ons	nous	**envoy**ions
vous	**envoy**ez	vous	**envoy**iez
ils	**envoi**ent	ils	**envoy**aient

		FUTURE	
		j'	enverrai
		tu	enverras
		il	enverra
		nous	enverrons
		vous	enverrez
		ils	enverront

IMPERATIVE		CONDITIONAL	
	envoie	j'	enverrais
	envoyons	tu	enverrais
	envoyez	il	enverrait
		nous	enverrions
		vous	enverriez
		ils	enverraient

envoyer 40

to send

PAST HISTORIC		PRESENT SUBJUNCTIVE	
j'	**envoy**ai	j'	**envoie**
tu	**envoy**as	tu	**envoies**
il	**envoy**a	il	**envoie**
nous	**envoy**âmes	nous	**envoy**ions
vous	**envoy**âtes	vous	**envoy**iez
ils	**envoy**èrent	ils	**envoient**

PERFECT		PAST SUBJUNCTIVE	
j'	**ai envoyé**	j'	**envoy**asse
tu	**as envoyé**	tu	**envoy**asses
il	**a envoyé**	il	**envoy**ât
nous	**avons envoyé**	nous	**envoy**assions
vous	**avez envoyé**	vous	**envoy**assiez
ils	**ont envoyé**	ils	**envoy**assent

CONSTRUCTIONS

envoyer chercher qn/qch   to send for sb/sth

41 espérer

to hope *also* **accélérer**
to accelerate

PRESENT PARTICIPLE
espérant

céder
to give up

PAST PARTICIPLE
espéré

compléter
to complete

PRESENT

j'	**espère**
tu	**espères**
il	**espère**
nous	**espérons**
vous	**espérez**
ils	**espèrent**

IMPERFECT

j'	**espérais**
tu	**espérais**
il	**espérait**
nous	**espérions**
vous	**espériez**
ils	**espéraient**

FUTURE

j'	**espérerai**
tu	**espéreras**
il	**espérera**
nous	**espérerons**
vous	**espérerez**
ils	**espéreront**

IMPERATIVE

espère
espérons
espérez

CONDITIONAL

j'	**espérerais**
tu	**espérerais**
il	**espérerait**
nous	**espérerions**
vous	**espéreriez**
ils	**espéreraient**

régler
to settle

sécher
to dry

PAST HISTORIC
j'	**espér**ai
tu	**espér**as
il	**espér**a
nous	**espér**âmes
vous	**espér**âtes
ils	**espér**èrent

PRESENT SUBJUNCTIVE
j'	**espère**
tu	**espères**
il	**espère**
nous	**espér**ions
vous	**espér**iez
ils	**espèrent**

PERFECT
j'	**ai espéré**
tu	**as espéré**
il	**a espéré**
nous	**avons espéré**
vous	**avez espéré**
ils	**ont espéré**

PAST SUBJUNCTIVE
j'	**espér**asse
tu	**espér**asses
il	**espér**ât
nous	**espér**assions
vous	**espér**assiez
ils	**espér**assent

CONSTRUCTIONS
espérer faire qch to hope to do sth
viendra-t-il? – je l'espère (bien) will he come? – I
(certainly) hope so
j'espère bien n'avoir rien oublié I hope I haven't
forgotten anything

42 être
to be

PRESENT PARTICIPLE
étant

PAST PARTICIPLE
été

PRESENT		IMPERFECT	
je	suis	j'	étais
tu	es	tu	étais
il	est	il	était
nous	sommes	nous	étions
vous	êtes	vous	étiez
ils	sont	ils	étaient

		FUTURE	
		je	serai
		tu	seras
		il	sera
		nous	serons
		vous	serez
		ils	seront

IMPERATIVE	CONDITIONAL	
sois	je	serais
soyons	tu	serais
soyez	il	serait
	nous	serions
	vous	seriez
	ils	seraient

PAST HISTORIC		PRESENT SUBJUNCTIVE	
je	fus	je	sois
tu	fus	tu	sois
il	fut	il	soit
nous	fûmes	nous	soyons
vous	fûtes	vous	soyez
ils	furent	ils	soient

PERFECT		PAST SUBJUNCTIVE	
j'	**ai** été	je	fusse
tu	**as** été	tu	fusses
il	**a** été	il	fût
nous	**avons** été	nous	fussions
vous	**avez** été	vous	fussiez
ils	**ont** été	ils	fussent

CONSTRUCTIONS

il est peintre he's a painter

quel jour sommes-nous? – nous sommes le 12 mars
what's today's date? – it's March 12th

à qui est ce cahier? – il est à elle whose jotter is this? –
it's hers

43 faire
to do; to make   *also* **contrefaire**
to forge

PRESENT PARTICIPLE
faisant

défaire
to undo

PAST PARTICIPLE
fait

refaire
to redo

PRESENT		IMPERFECT	
je	**fais**	je	**faisais**
tu	**fais**	tu	**faisais**
il	**fait**	il	**faisait**
nous	**faisons**	nous	**faisions**
vous	**faites**	vous	**faisiez**
ils	**font**	ils	**faisaient**

		FUTURE	
		je	**ferai**
		tu	**feras**
		il	**fera**
		nous	**ferons**
		vous	**ferez**
		ils	**feront**

IMPERATIVE	CONDITIONAL	
fais	je	**ferais**
faisons	tu	**ferais**
faites	il	**ferait**
	nous	**ferions**
	vous	**feriez**
	ils	**feraient**

satisfaire
to satisfy

to do; to make

PAST HISTORIC		PRESENT SUBJUNCTIVE	
je	fis	je	fasse
tu	fis	tu	fasses
il	fit	il	fasse
nous	fîmes	nous	fassions
vous	fîtes	vous	fassiez
ils	firent	ils	fassent

PERFECT		PAST SUBJUNCTIVE	
j'	ai fait	je	fisse
tu	as fait	tu	fisses
il	a fait	il	fît
nous	avons fait	nous	fissions
vous	avez fait	vous	fissiez
ils	ont fait	ils	fissent

CONSTRUCTIONS

faire la vaisselle/la cuisine   to do the dishes/the cooking
faire une promenade/des courses   to go for a walk/go shopping
il fait beau/du vent   it's nice/windy
faire faire qch   to have sth done *or* made

44 falloir
to be necessary

PRESENT PARTICIPLE
not used

PAST PARTICIPLE
fallu

PRESENT	*IMPERFECT*
il faut	**il fallait**
	FUTURE
	il faudra
IMPERATIVE	*CONDITIONAL*
not used	**il faudrait**

PAST HISTORIC il **fall**ut	*PRESENT SUBJUNCTIVE* il **faille**
PERFECT il **a fall**u	*PAST SUBJUNCTIVE* il **fall**ût

CONSTRUCTIONS

il lui faut quelqu'un pour l'aider   he needs somebody to help him

il faut qu'il parte   he'll have to *or* has to go

il faut être prudent   you have to be careful

45 finir

to finish

also agir
to act

PRESENT PARTICIPLE
finissant

bâtir
to build

PAST PARTICIPLE
fini

durcir
to harden

PRESENT		IMPERFECT	
je	**finis**	je	**finissais**
tu	**finis**	tu	**finissais**
il	**finit**	il	**finissait**
nous	**finissons**	nous	**finissions**
vous	**finissez**	vous	**finissiez**
ils	**finissent**	ils	**finissaient**

		FUTURE	
		je	**finirai**
		tu	**finiras**
		il	**finira**
		nous	**finirons**
		vous	**finirez**
		ils	**finiront**

IMPERATIVE	CONDITIONAL	
finis	je	**finirais**
finissons	tu	**finirais**
finissez	il	**finirait**
	nous	**finirions**
	vous	**finiriez**
	ils	**finiraient**

guérir
to heal

to finish

réunir
to reunite

PAST HISTORIC		PRESENT SUBJUNCTIVE	
je	**fin**is	je	**fin**isse
tu	**fin**is	tu	**fin**isses
il	**fin**it	il	**fin**isse
nous	**fin**îmes	nous	**fin**issions
vous	**fin**îtes	vous	**fin**issiez
ils	**fin**irent	ils	**fin**issent

PERFECT		PAST SUBJUNCTIVE	
j'	**ai fin**i	je	**fin**isse
tu	**as fin**i	tu	**fin**isses
il	**a fin**i	il	**fin**ît
nous	**avons fin**i	nous	**fin**issions
vous	**avez fin**i	vous	**fin**issiez
ils	**ont fin**i	ils	**fin**issent

CONSTRUCTIONS
finir de faire qch   to finish doing sth
il a fini par comprendre   he finally understood
tout finira par s'arranger   everything will work out in the end
le film finit bien   the film has a happy ending

46 fuir

to flee

also **s'enfuir**
to run away

PRESENT PARTICIPLE
fuyant

PAST PARTICIPLE
fui

PRESENT		IMPERFECT	
je	**fuis**	je	**fuyais**
tu	**fuis**	tu	**fuyais**
il	**fuit**	il	**fuyait**
nous	**fuyons**	nous	**fuyions**
vous	**fuyez**	vous	**fuyiez**
ils	**fuient**	ils	**fuyaient**

		FUTURE	
		je	**fuirai**
		tu	**fuiras**
		il	**fuira**
		nous	**fuirons**
		vous	**fuirez**
		ils	**fuiront**

IMPERATIVE	CONDITIONAL	
fuis	je	**fuirais**
fuyons	tu	**fuirais**
fuyez	il	**fuirait**
	nous	**fuirions**
	vous	**fuiriez**
	ils	**fuiraient**

PAST HISTORIC	*PRESENT SUBJUNCTIVE*
je **fuis**	je **fuie**
tu **fuis**	tu **fuies**
il **fuit**	il **fuie**
nous **fuîmes**	nous **fuyions**
vous **fuîtes**	vous **fuyiez**
ils **fuirent**	ils **fuient**
PERFECT	*PAST SUBJUNCTIVE*
j' **ai fui**	je **fuisse**
tu **as fui**	tu **fuisses**
il **a fui**	il **fuît**
nous **avons fui**	nous **fuissions**
vous **avez fui**	vous **fuissiez**
ils **ont fui**	ils **fuissent**

CONSTRUCTIONS

fuir devant un danger/ses responsabilités to run away
from danger/one's responsibilities

47 haïr
to hate

PRESENT PARTICIPLE
haïssant

PAST PARTICIPLE
haï

PRESENT		*IMPERFECT*	
je	hais	je	**haïssais**
tu	hais	tu	**haïssais**
il	hait	il	**haïssait**
nous	**haïssons**	nous	**haïssions**
vous	**haïssez**	vous	**haïssiez**
ils	**haïssent**	ils	**haïssaient**

		FUTURE	
		je	**haïrai**
		tu	**haïras**
		il	**haïra**
		nous	**haïrons**
		vous	**haïrez**
		ils	**haïront**

IMPERATIVE		*CONDITIONAL*	
	hais	je	**haïrais**
	haïssons	tu	**haïrais**
	haïssez	il	**haïrait**
		nous	**haïrions**
		vous	**haïriez**
		ils	**haïraient**

PAST HISTORIC
je	**haïs**
tu	**haïs**
il	**haït**
nous	**haïmes**
vous	**haïtes**
ils	**haïrent**

PERFECT
j'	**ai**	haï
tu	**as**	haï
il	**a**	haï
nous	**avons**	haï
vous	**avez**	haï
ils	**ont**	haï

PRESENT SUBJUNCTIVE
je	**haïsse**
tu	**haïsses**
il	**haïsse**
nous	**haïssions**
vous	**haïssiez**
ils	**haïssent**

PAST SUBJUNCTIVE
je	**haïsse**
tu	**haïsses**
il	**haït**
nous	**haïssions**
vous	**haïssiez**
ils	**haïssent**

48 interdire
to forbid

also **contredire**
to contradict

PRESENT PARTICIPLE
interdisant

prédire
to predict

PAST PARTICIPLE
interdit

PRESENT		*IMPERFECT*	
j'	**interdis**	j'	**interdisais**
tu	**interdis**	tu	**interdisais**
il	**interdit**	il	**interdisait**
nous	**interdisons**	nous	**interdisions**
vous	**interdisez**	vous	**interdisiez**
ils	**interdisent**	ils	**interdisaient**

		FUTURE	
		j'	**interdirai**
		tu	**interdiras**
		il	**interdira**
		nous	**interdirons**
		vous	**interdirez**
		ils	**interdiront**

IMPERATIVE	*CONDITIONAL*	
interdis	j'	**interdirais**
interdisons	tu	**interdirais**
interdisez	il	**interdirait**
	nous	**interdirions**
	vous	**interdiriez**
	ils	**interdiraient**

PAST HISTORIC		PRESENT SUBJUNCTIVE	
j'	**interdis**	j'	**interdise**
tu	**interdis**	tu	**interdises**
il	**interdit**	il	**interdise**
nous	**interdîmes**	nous	**interdisions**
vous	**interdîtes**	vous	**interdisiez**
ils	**interdirent**	ils	**interdisent**

PERFECT		PAST SUBJUNCTIVE	
j'	**ai interdit**	j'	**interdisse**
tu	**as interdit**	tu	**interdisses**
il	**a interdit**	il	**interdît**
nous	**avons interdit**	nous	**interdissions**
vous	**avez interdit**	vous	**interdissiez**
ils	**ont interdit**	ils	**interdissent**

CONSTRUCTIONS

interdire à qn de faire qch   to forbid sb to do sth
il m'a interdit l'alcool/le tabac   he's forbidden me to drink/smoke
il est interdit de fumer   smoking is prohibited
stationnement interdit   no parking

49 introduire
to introduce

PRESENT PARTICIPLE
introduisant

PAST PARTICIPLE
introduit

PRESENT		*IMPERFECT*	
j'	**introdui**s	j'	**introdui**sais
tu	**introdui**s	tu	**introdui**sais
il	**introdui**t	il	**introdui**sait
nous	**introdui**sons	nous	**introdui**sions
vous	**introdui**sez	vous	**introdui**siez
ils	**introdui**sent	ils	**introdui**saient

		FUTURE	
		j'	**introdui**rai
		tu	**introdui**ras
		il	**introdui**ra
		nous	**introdui**rons
		vous	**introdui**rez
		ils	**introdui**ront

IMPERATIVE	*CONDITIONAL*	
introduis	j'	**introdui**rais
introduisons	tu	**introdui**rais
introduisez	il	**introdui**rait
	nous	**introdui**rions
	vous	**introdui**riez
	ils	**introdui**raient

to introduce

PAST HISTORIC		PRESENT SUBJUNCTIVE	
j'	**introduisis**	j'	**introduise**
tu	**introduisis**	tu	**introduises**
il	**introduisit**	il	**introduise**
nous	**introduisîmes**	nous	**introduisions**
vous	**introduisîtes**	vous	**introduisiez**
ils	**introduisirent**	ils	**introduisent**

PERFECT		PAST SUBJUNCTIVE	
j'	**ai introduit**	j'	**introduisisse**
tu	**as introduit**	tu	**introduisisses**
il	**a introduit**	il	**introduisît**
nous	**avons introduit**	nous	**introduisissions**
vous	**avez introduit**	vous	**introduisissiez**
ils	**ont introduit**	ils	**introduisissent**

CONSTRUCTIONS

il a introduit sa clef dans la serrure he inserted his key in the lock

il m'a introduit dans le salon he showed me into the lounge

s'introduire dans une pièce to get into a room

50 jeter

to throw

also **breveter**
to patent

PRESENT PARTICIPLE
jetant

étiqueter
to label

PAST PARTICIPLE
jeté

feuilleter
to leaf through

PRESENT		IMPERFECT	
je	**jette**	je	**jetais**
tu	**jettes**	tu	**jetais**
il	**jette**	il	**jetait**
nous	**jetons**	nous	**jetions**
vous	**jetez**	vous	**jetiez**
ils	**jettent**	ils	**jetaient**

		FUTURE	
		je	**jetterai**
		tu	**jetteras**
		il	**jettera**
		nous	**jetterons**
		vous	**jetterez**
		ils	**jetteront**

IMPERATIVE	CONDITIONAL	
jette	je	**jetterais**
jetons	tu	**jetterais**
jetez	il	**jetterait**
	nous	**jetterions**
	vous	**jetteriez**
	ils	**jetteraient**

projeter
to plan

rejeter
to reject

PAST HISTORIC		PRESENT SUBJUNCTIVE	
je	**jet**ai	je	**jett**e
tu	**jet**as	tu	**jett**es
il	**jet**a	il	**jett**e
nous	**jet**âmes	nous	**jet**ions
vous	**jet**âtes	vous	**jet**iez
ils	**jet**èrent	ils	**jett**ent

PERFECT		PAST SUBJUNCTIVE	
j'	**ai jeté**	je	**jet**asse
tu	**as jeté**	tu	**jet**asses
il	**a jeté**	il	**jet**ât
nous	**avons jeté**	nous	**jet**assions
vous	**avez jeté**	vous	**jet**assiez
ils	**ont jeté**	ils	**jet**assent

CONSTRUCTIONS

jeter qch à qn   to throw sth to sb; to throw sth at sb
jeter qch par terre/par la fenêtre   to throw sth down/out of the window
jeter qn dehors *or* **à la porte**   to throw sb out

51 joindre

to join

also **adjoindre**
to attach

PRESENT PARTICIPLE
joignant

rejoindre
to rejoin

PAST PARTICIPLE
joint

PRESENT		IMPERFECT	
je	joins	je	joignais
tu	joins	tu	joignais
il	joint	il	joignait
nous	joignons	nous	joignions
vous	joignez	vous	joigniez
ils	joignent	ils	joignaient

FUTURE	
je	**joindr**ai
tu	**joindr**as
il	**joindr**a
nous	**joindr**ons
vous	**joindr**ez
ils	**joindr**ont

IMPERATIVE
joins
joignons
joignez

CONDITIONAL	
je	**joindr**ais
tu	**joindr**ais
il	**joindr**ait
nous	**joindr**ions
vous	**joindr**iez
ils	**joindr**aient

PAST HISTORIC		PRESENT SUBJUNCTIVE	
je	joignis	je	joigne
tu	joignis	tu	joignes
il	joignit	il	joigne
nous	joignîmes	nous	joignions
vous	joignîtes	vous	joigniez
ils	joignirent	ils	joignent

PERFECT		PAST SUBJUNCTIVE	
j'	**ai** joint	je	joignisse
tu	**as** joint	tu	joignisses
il	**a** joint	il	joignît
nous	**avons** joint	nous	joignissions
vous	**avez** joint	vous	joignissiez
ils	**ont** joint	ils	joignissent

CONSTRUCTIONS
joindre les mains   to clasp one's hands (together)
voir la lettre ci-jointe   see the enclosed letter
elle joint l'intelligence à la beauté   she combines intelligence and beauty
se joindre à   to join

52 lever
to lift

also amener
to bring

PRESENT PARTICIPLE
levant

élever
to raise

PAST PARTICIPLE
levé

enlever
to remove

PRESENT		IMPERFECT	
je	**lè**ve	je	**lev**ais
tu	**lè**ves	tu	**lev**ais
il	**lè**ve	il	**lev**ait
nous	**lev**ons	nous	**lev**ions
vous	**lev**ez	vous	**lev**iez
ils	**lè**vent	ils	**lev**aient

FUTURE
je	**lè**verai
tu	**lè**veras
il	**lè**vera
nous	**lè**verons
vous	**lè**verez
ils	**lè**veront

IMPERATIVE	CONDITIONAL	
lève	je	**lè**verais
levons	tu	**lè**verais
levez	il	**lè**verait
	nous	**lè**verions
	vous	**lè**veriez
	ils	**lè**veraient

to lift

mener
   to lead

peser
   to weigh

PAST HISTORIC		*PRESENT SUBJUNCTIVE*	
je	**lev**ai	je	**lève**
tu	**lev**as	tu	**lèves**
il	**lev**a	il	**lève**
nous	**lev**âmes	nous	**lev**ions
vous	**lev**âtes	vous	**lev**iez
ils	**lev**èrent	ils	**lèv**ent

PERFECT		*PAST SUBJUNCTIVE*	
j'	**ai levé**	je	**lev**asse
tu	**as levé**	tu	**lev**asses
il	**a levé**	il	**lev**ât
nous	**avons levé**	nous	**lev**assions
vous	**avez levé**	vous	**lev**assiez
ils	**ont levé**	ils	**lev**assent

CONSTRUCTIONS
lever les yeux to look up
levez la main! put your hand up!
lever son verre à qn to raise one's glass to sb
se lever to get up; to rise
le jour/la brume se lève day breaks/the mist is clearing

53 lire

to read   *also* **élire**
                               to elect

PRESENT PARTICIPLE
lisant

PAST PARTICIPLE
lu

PRESENT		*IMPERFECT*	
je	**lis**	je	**lisais**
tu	**lis**	tu	**lisais**
il	**lit**	il	**lisait**
nous	**lisons**	nous	**lisions**
vous	**lisez**	vous	**lisiez**
ils	**lisent**	ils	**lisaient**

		FUTURE	
		je	**lirai**
		tu	**liras**
		il	**lira**
		nous	**lirons**
		vous	**lirez**
		ils	**liront**

IMPERATIVE	*CONDITIONAL*	
lis	je	**lirais**
lisons	tu	**lirais**
lisez	il	**lirait**
	nous	**lirions**
	vous	**liriez**
	ils	**liraient**

PAST HISTORIC		PRESENT SUBJUNCTIVE	
je	lus	je	lise
tu	lus	tu	lises
il	lut	il	lise
nous	lûmes	nous	lisions
vous	lûtes	vous	lisiez
ils	lurent	ils	lisent

PERFECT		PAST SUBJUNCTIVE	
j'	ai lu	je	lusse
tu	as lu	tu	lusses
il	a lu	il	lût
nous	avons lu	nous	lussions
vous	avez lu	vous	lussiez
ils	ont lu	ils	lussent

CONSTRUCTIONS

je lui ai lu une histoire I read him a story
c'est un livre à lire it's a book you should read

54 manger

to eat

also **arranger**
to arrange

PRESENT PARTICIPLE
mangeant

bouger
to move

PAST PARTICIPLE
mangé

dégager
to clear

PRESENT		*IMPERFECT*	
je	**mange**	je	**mangeais**
tu	**manges**	tu	**mangeais**
il	**mange**	il	**mangeait**
nous	**mangeons**	nous	**mangions**
vous	**mangez**	vous	**mangiez**
ils	**mangent**	ils	**mangeaient**

		FUTURE	
		je	**mangerai**
		tu	**mangeras**
		il	**mangera**
		nous	**mangerons**
		vous	**mangerez**
		ils	**mangeront**

IMPERATIVE		*CONDITIONAL*	
	mange	je	**mangerais**
	mangeons	tu	**mangerais**
	mangez	il	**mangerait**
		nous	**mangerions**
		vous	**mangeriez**
		ils	**mangeraient**

diriger
to manage

loger
to accommodate

manger
to eat

PAST HISTORIC		PRESENT SUBJUNCTIVE	
je	**mangeai**	je	**mange**
tu	**mangeas**	tu	**manges**
il	**mangea**	il	**mange**
nous	**mangeâmes**	nous	**mangions**
vous	**mangeâtes**	vous	**mangiez**
ils	**mangèrent**	ils	**mangent**

PERFECT		PAST SUBJUNCTIVE	
j'	**ai mangé**	je	**mangeasse**
tu	**as mangé**	tu	**mangeasses**
il	**a mangé**	il	**mangeât**
nous	**avons mangé**	nous	**mangeassions**
vous	**avez mangé**	vous	**mangeassiez**
ils	**ont mangé**	ils	**mangeassent**

CONSTRUCTIONS
manger comme quatre   to eat like a horse
est-ce que ça se mange?   is it edible?

55 maudire
to curse

PRESENT PARTICIPLE
maudissant

PAST PARTICIPLE
maudit

PRESENT
je	**maud**is
tu	**maud**is
il	**maud**it
nous	**maud**issons
vous	**maud**issez
ils	**maud**issent

IMPERFECT
je	**maud**issais
tu	**maud**issais
il	**maud**issait
nous	**maud**issions
vous	**maud**issiez
ils	**maud**issaient

FUTURE
je	**maud**irai
tu	**maud**iras
il	**maud**ira
nous	**maud**irons
vous	**maud**irez
ils	**maud**iront

IMPERATIVE
maudis
maudissons
maudissez

CONDITIONAL
je	**maud**irais
tu	**maud**irais
il	**maud**irait
nous	**maud**irions
vous	**maud**iriez
ils	**maud**iraient

PAST HISTORIC

je	maudis
tu	maudis
il	maudit
nous	maudîmes
vous	maudîtes
ils	maudirent

PRESENT SUBJUNCTIVE

je	maudisse
tu	maudisses
il	maudisse
nous	maudissions
vous	maudissiez
ils	maudissent

PERFECT

j'	ai maudit
tu	as maudit
il	a maudit
nous	avons maudit
vous	avez maudit
ils	ont maudit

PAST SUBJUNCTIVE

je	maudisse
tu	maudisses
il	maudît
nous	maudissions
vous	maudissiez
ils	maudissent

CONSTRUCTIONS

ce maudit stylo ne marche pas! this blasted pen won't work!

56 mettre

to put

also admettre
to admit

PRESENT PARTICIPLE
mettant

commettre
to commit

PAST PARTICIPLE
mis

émettre
to emit

PRESENT

je	**mets**
tu	**mets**
il	**met**
nous	**mett**ons
vous	**mett**ez
ils	**mett**ent

IMPERFECT

je	**mett**ais
tu	**mett**ais
il	**mett**ait
nous	**mett**ions
vous	**mett**iez
ils	**mett**aient

FUTURE

je	**mett**rai
tu	**mett**ras
il	**mett**ra
nous	**mett**rons
vous	**mett**rez
ils	**mett**ront

IMPERATIVE

mets
mettons
mettez

CONDITIONAL

je	**mett**rais
tu	**mett**rais
il	**mett**rait
nous	**mett**rions
vous	**mett**riez
ils	**mett**raient

soumettre
to submit

transmettre
to transmit

PAST HISTORIC		PRESENT SUBJUNCTIVE	
je	**mis**	je	**mette**
tu	**mis**	tu	**mettes**
il	**mit**	il	**mette**
nous	**mîmes**	nous	**mettions**
vous	**mîtes**	vous	**mettiez**
ils	**mirent**	ils	**mettent**

PERFECT		PAST SUBJUNCTIVE	
j'	**ai** mis	je	**misse**
tu	**as** mis	tu	**misses**
il	**a** mis	il	**mît**
nous	**avons** mis	nous	**missions**
vous	**avez** mis	vous	**missiez**
ils	**ont** mis	ils	**missent**

CONSTRUCTIONS

j'ai mis 2 heures à le faire   I took 2 hours to do it
elle n'a rien à se mettre   she's nothing to wear
se mettre à faire qch   to start doing sth
se mettre au travail   to set to work

57 monter
to go up

PRESENT PARTICIPLE
montant

PAST PARTICIPLE
monté

PRESENT		*IMPERFECT*	
je	**monte**	je	**montais**
tu	**montes**	tu	**montais**
il	**monte**	il	**montait**
nous	**montons**	nous	**montions**
vous	**montez**	vous	**montiez**
ils	**montent**	ils	**montaient**

		FUTURE	
		je	**monterai**
		tu	**monteras**
		il	**montera**
		nous	**monterons**
		vous	**monterez**
		ils	**monteront**

IMPERATIVE	*CONDITIONAL*	
monte	je	**monterais**
montons	tu	**monterais**
montez	il	**monterait**
	nous	**monterions**
	vous	**monteriez**
	ils	**monteraient**

monter 57

to go up

PAST HISTORIC
- je **mont**ai
- tu **mont**as
- il **mont**a
- nous **mont**âmes
- vous **mont**âtes
- ils **mont**èrent

PRESENT SUBJUNCTIVE
- je **mont**e
- tu **mont**es
- il **mont**e
- nous **mont**ions
- vous **mont**iez
- ils **mont**ent

PERFECT
- je suis **mont**é
- tu es **mont**é
- il est **mont**é
- nous sommes **mont**és
- vous êtes **mont**é(s)
- ils sont **mont**és

PAST SUBJUNCTIVE
- je **mont**asse
- tu **mont**asses
- il **mont**ât
- nous **mont**assions
- vous **mont**assiez
- ils **mont**assent

CONSTRUCTIONS

monter dans un train/un avion   to get on a train/plane
monter en voiture   to get into a car
monter à bicyclette/cheval   to get on a bicycle/horse; to ride a bicycle/horse
il a monté la valise   he took the case up

58 mordre
to bite

also **tordre**
to twist

PRESENT PARTICIPLE
mordant

PAST PARTICIPLE
mordu

PRESENT
je **mords**
tu **mords**
il **mord**
nous **mordons**
vous **mordez**
ils **mordent**

IMPERFECT
je **mordais**
tu **mordais**
il **mordait**
nous **mordions**
vous **mordiez**
ils **mordaient**

FUTURE
je **mordrai**
tu **mordras**
il **mordra**
nous **mordrons**
vous **mordrez**
ils **mordront**

IMPERATIVE
mords
mordons
mordez

CONDITIONAL
je **mordrais**
tu **mordrais**
il **mordrait**
nous **mordrions**
vous **mordriez**
ils **mordraient**

to bite

PAST HISTORIC

je	**mord**is
tu	**mord**is
il	**mord**it
nous	**mord**îmes
vous	**mord**îtes
ils	**mord**irent

PRESENT SUBJUNCTIVE

je	**mord**e
tu	**mord**es
il	**mord**e
nous	**mord**ions
vous	**mord**iez
ils	**mord**ent

PERFECT

j'	**ai mord**u
tu	**as mord**u
il	**a mord**u
nous	**avons mord**u
vous	**avez mord**u
ils	**ont mord**u

PAST SUBJUNCTIVE

je	**mord**isse
tu	**mord**isses
il	**mord**ît
nous	**mord**issions
vous	**mord**issiez
ils	**mord**issent

CONSTRUCTIONS

mordre qn à la main   to bite sb's hand
mordre dans une pomme   to bite into an apple
mordu de football   mad keen on football
mordre à l'hameçon   to rise to the bait

59 moudre
to grind

PRESENT PARTICIPLE
moulant

PAST PARTICIPLE
moulu

PRESENT		IMPERFECT	
je	**mouds**	je	moulais
tu	**mouds**	tu	moulais
il	**moud**	il	moulait
nous	**moulons**	nous	moulions
vous	**moulez**	vous	mouliez
ils	**moulent**	ils	moulaient

		FUTURE	
		je	**moudrai**
		tu	**moudras**
		il	**moudra**
		nous	**moudrons**
		vous	**moudrez**
		ils	**moudront**

IMPERATIVE		CONDITIONAL	
	mouds	je	**moudrais**
	moulons	tu	**moudrais**
	moulez	il	**moudrait**
		nous	**moudrions**
		vous	**moudriez**
		ils	**moudraient**

PAST HISTORIC		PRESENT SUBJUNCTIVE	
je	moulus	je	moule
tu	moulus	tu	moules
il	moulut	il	moule
nous	moulûmes	nous	moulions
vous	moulûtes	vous	mouliez
ils	moulurent	ils	moulent

PERFECT		PAST SUBJUNCTIVE	
j'	**ai** moulu	je	moulusse
tu	**as** moulu	tu	moulusses
il	**a** moulu	il	moulût
nous	**avons** moulu	nous	moulussions
vous	**avez** moulu	vous	moulussiez
ils	**ont** moulu	ils	moulussent

CONSTRUCTIONS

je l'aimerais moulu très fin, s'il vous plaît   I'd like it very finely ground, please

60 mourir
to die

PRESENT PARTICIPLE
mourant

PAST PARTICIPLE
mort

PRESENT		IMPERFECT	
je	**meurs**	je	**mour**ais
tu	**meurs**	tu	**mour**ais
il	**meurt**	il	**mour**ait
nous	**mour**ons	nous	**mour**ions
vous	**mour**ez	vous	**mour**iez
ils	**meurent**	ils	**mour**aient

	FUTURE	
	je	**mour**rai
	tu	**mour**ras
	il	**mour**ra
	nous	**mour**rons
	vous	**mour**rez
	ils	**mour**ront

IMPERATIVE	CONDITIONAL	
meurs	je	**mour**rais
mourons	tu	**mour**rais
mourez	il	**mour**rait
	nous	**mour**rions
	vous	**mour**riez
	ils	**mour**raient

to die

PAST HISTORIC		PRESENT SUBJUNCTIVE	
je	**mour**us	je	**meure**
tu	**mour**us	tu	**meures**
il	**mour**ut	il	**meure**
nous	**mour**ûmes	nous	**mour**ions
vous	**mour**ûtes	vous	**mour**iez
ils	**mour**urent	ils	**meurent**

PERFECT		PAST SUBJUNCTIVE	
je	suis mort	je	**mour**usse
tu	es mort	tu	**mour**usses
il	est mort	il	**mour**ût
nous	sommes mort	nous	**mour**ussions
vous	êtes mort(s)	vous	**mour**ussiez
ils	sont morts	ils	**mour**ussent

CONSTRUCTIONS

il est mort   he's dead
il est mort en 1960   he died in 1960
mourir de faim/froid   to die of hunger/cold
être mort de peur   to be scared to death
mourir d'envie de faire qch   to be dying to do sth

61 mouvoir
to move

PRESENT PARTICIPLE
mouvant

PAST PARTICIPLE
mû (*NB:* **mue, mus, mues**)

PRESENT		*IMPERFECT*	
je	**meus**	je	**mouv**ais
tu	**meus**	tu	**mouv**ais
il	**meut**	il	**mouv**ait
nous	**mouv**ons	nous	**mouv**ions
vous	**mouv**ez	vous	**mouv**iez
ils	**meuv**ent	ils	**mouv**aient

		FUTURE	
		je	**mouv**rai
		tu	**mouv**ras
		il	**mouv**ra
		nous	**mouv**rons
		vous	**mouv**rez
		ils	**mouv**ront

IMPERATIVE		*CONDITIONAL*	
	meus	je	**mouv**rais
	mouvons	tu	**mouv**rais
	mouvez	il	**mouv**rait
		nous	**mouv**rions
		vous	**mouv**riez
		ils	**mouv**raient

PAST HISTORIC		PRESENT SUBJUNCTIVE	
je	mus	je	meuve
tu	mus	tu	meuves
il	mut	il	meuve
nous	mûmes	nous	**mouv**ions
vous	mûtes	vous	**mouv**iez
ils	murent	ils	meuvent

PERFECT		PAST SUBJUNCTIVE	
j′	**ai** mû	je	musse
tu	**as** mû	tu	musses
il	**a** mû	il	mût
nous	**avons** mû	nous	mussions
vous	**avez** mû	vous	mussiez
ils	**ont** mû	ils	mussent

CONSTRUCTIONS
il a de la peine à se mouvoir he has difficulty in moving

62 naître

to be born

PRESENT PARTICIPLE
naissant

PAST PARTICIPLE
né

PRESENT

je	**nais**
tu	**nais**
il	**naît**
nous	**naissons**
vous	**naissez**
ils	**naissent**

IMPERFECT

je	**naissais**
tu	**naissais**
il	**naissait**
nous	**naissions**
vous	**naissiez**
ils	**naissaient**

FUTURE

je	**naîtrai**
tu	**naîtras**
il	**naîtra**
nous	**naîtrons**
vous	**naîtrez**
ils	**naîtront**

IMPERATIVE

nais
naissons
naissez

CONDITIONAL

je	**naîtrais**
tu	**naîtrais**
il	**naîtrait**
nous	**naîtrions**
vous	**naîtriez**
ils	**naîtraient**

PAST HISTORIC		PRESENT SUBJUNCTIVE	
je	naquis	je	naisse
tu	naquis	tu	naisses
il	naquit	il	naisse
nous	naquîmes	nous	naissions
vous	naquîtes	vous	naissiez
ils	naquirent	ils	naissent

PERFECT		PAST SUBJUNCTIVE	
je	suis né	je	naquisse
tu	es né	tu	naquisses
il	est né	il	naquît
nous	sommes nés	nous	naquissions
vous	êtes né(s)	vous	naquissiez
ils	sont nés	ils	naquissent

CONSTRUCTIONS

je suis né le 5 mars I was born on 5th March
il naît plus de filles que de garçons there are more girls born than boys
faire naître des soupçons to arouse suspicion

63 nettoyer
to clean

also **aboyer**
to bark

PRESENT PARTICIPLE
nettoyant

appuyer
to lean

PAST PARTICIPLE
nettoyé

employer
to use

PRESENT
je	nettoie
tu	nettoies
il	nettoie
nous	**nettoy**ons
vous	**nettoy**ez
ils	nettoient

IMPERFECT
je	**nettoy**ais
tu	**nettoy**ais
il	**nettoy**ait
nous	**nettoy**ions
vous	**nettoy**iez
ils	**nettoy**aient

FUTURE
je	nettoierai
tu	nettoieras
il	nettoiera
nous	nettoierons
vous	nettoierez
ils	nettoieront

IMPERATIVE
nettoie
nettoyons
nettoyez

CONDITIONAL
je	nettoierais
tu	nettoierais
il	nettoierait
nous	nettoierions
vous	nettoieriez
ils	nettoieraient

nettoyer 63
to clean

ennuyer
to bore

essuyer
to wipe

PAST HISTORIC
- je **nettoy**ai
- tu **nettoy**as
- il **nettoy**a
- nous **nettoy**âmes
- vous **nettoy**âtes
- ils **nettoy**èrent

PRESENT SUBJUNCTIVE
- je **nettoie**
- tu **nettoies**
- il **nettoie**
- nous **nettoy**ions
- vous **nettoy**iez
- ils **nettoient**

PERFECT
- j' **ai nettoy**é
- tu **as nettoy**é
- il **a nettoy**é
- nous **avons nettoy**é
- vous **avez nettoy**é
- ils **ont nettoy**é

PAST SUBJUNCTIVE
- je **nettoy**asse
- tu **nettoy**asses
- il **nettoy**ât
- nous **nettoy**assions
- vous **nettoy**assiez
- ils **nettoy**assent

CONSTRUCTIONS
nettoyer à sec to dry-clean

64 obtenir

to get

PRESENT PARTICIPLE
obtenant

PAST PARTICIPLE
obtenu

PRESENT		*IMPERFECT*	
j'	obtiens	j'	**obten**ais
tu	obtiens	tu	**obten**ais
il	obtient	il	**obten**ait
nous	**obten**ons	nous	**obten**ions
vous	**obten**ez	vous	**obten**iez
ils	obtiennent	ils	**obten**aient

		FUTURE	
		j'	obtiendrai
		tu	obtiendras
		il	obtiendra
		nous	obtiendrons
		vous	obtiendrez
		ils	obtiendront

IMPERATIVE		*CONDITIONAL*	
	obtiens	j'	obtiendrais
	obtenons	tu	obtiendrais
	obtenez	il	obtiendrait
		nous	obtiendrions
		vous	obtiendriez
		ils	obtiendraient

PAST HISTORIC		PRESENT SUBJUNCTIVE	
j'	obtins	j'	obtienne
tu	obtins	tu	obtiennes
il	obtint	il	obtienne
nous	obtînmes	nous	**obten**ions
vous	obtîntes	vous	**obten**iez
ils	obtinrent	ils	obtiennent

PERFECT		PAST SUBJUNCTIVE	
j'	**ai obten**u	j'	obtinsse
tu	**as obten**u	tu	obtinsses
il	**a obten**u	il	obtînt
nous	**avons obten**u	nous	obtinssions
vous	**avez obten**u	vous	obtinssiez
ils	**ont obten**u	ils	obtinssent

CONSTRUCTIONS

obtenir qch de qn   to get sth from sb
obtenir de qn qu'il fasse qch   to get sb to do sth

65 offrir

to offer   *also* **souffrir**
                        to suffer

PRESENT PARTICIPLE
offrant

PAST PARTICIPLE
offert

PRESENT		*IMPERFECT*	
j'	**offre**	j'	**offr**ais
tu	**offres**	tu	**offr**ais
il	**offre**	il	**offr**ait
nous	**offrons**	nous	**offr**ions
vous	**offrez**	vous	**offr**iez
ils	**offrent**	ils	**offr**aient

		FUTURE	
		j'	**offrir**ai
		tu	**offrir**as
		il	**offrir**a
		nous	**offrir**ons
		vous	**offrir**ez
		ils	**offrir**ont

IMPERATIVE		*CONDITIONAL*	
	offre	j'	**offrir**ais
	offrons	tu	**offrir**ais
	offrez	il	**offrir**ait
		nous	**offrir**ions
		vous	**offrir**iez
		ils	**offrir**aient

PAST HISTORIC		PRESENT SUBJUNCTIVE	
j'	**offris**	j'	**offre**
tu	**offris**	tu	**offres**
il	**offrit**	il	**offre**
nous	**offrîmes**	nous	**offrions**
vous	**offrîtes**	vous	**offriez**
ils	**offrirent**	ils	**offrent**

PERFECT		PAST SUBJUNCTIVE	
j'	**ai** offert	j'	**offrisse**
tu	**as** offert	tu	**offrisses**
il	**a** offert	il	**offrît**
nous	**avons** offert	nous	**offrissions**
vous	**avez** offert	vous	**offrissiez**
ils	**ont** offert	ils	**offrissent**

CONSTRUCTIONS

offrir qch à qn to give sb sth; to offer sb sth

offrir de faire qch to offer to do sth

s'offrir un bon repas/un disque to treat oneself to a good meal/a record

il s'est offert en otage/comme guide he volunteered to be *or* as a hostage/guide

66 ouvrir

to open   *also* **rouvrir**
                            to reopen

PRESENT PARTICIPLE
ouvrant

PAST PARTICIPLE
ouvert

PRESENT		*IMPERFECT*	
j'	**ouvre**	j'	**ouvrais**
tu	**ouvres**	tu	**ouvrais**
il	**ouvre**	il	**ouvrait**
nous	**ouvrons**	nous	**ouvrions**
vous	**ouvrez**	vous	**ouvriez**
ils	**ouvrent**	ils	**ouvraient**

		FUTURE	
		j'	**ouvrirai**
		tu	**ouvriras**
		il	**ouvrira**
		nous	**ouvrirons**
		vous	**ouvrirez**
		ils	**ouvriront**

IMPERATIVE		*CONDITIONAL*	
	ouvre	j'	**ouvrirais**
	ouvrons	tu	**ouvrirais**
	ouvrez	il	**ouvrirait**
		nous	**ouvririons**
		vous	**ouvririez**
		ils	**ouvriraient**

PAST HISTORIC		PRESENT SUBJUNCTIVE	
j'	**ouvris**	j'	**ouvre**
tu	**ouvris**	tu	**ouvres**
il	**ouvrit**	il	**ouvre**
nous	**ouvrîmes**	nous	**ouvrions**
vous	**ouvrîtes**	vous	**ouvriez**
ils	**ouvrirent**	ils	**ouvrent**

PERFECT		PAST SUBJUNCTIVE	
j'	**ai** ouvert	j'	**ouvrisse**
tu	**as** ouvert	tu	**ouvrisses**
il	**a** ouvert	il	**ouvrît**
nous	**avons** ouvert	nous	**ouvrissions**
vous	**avez** ouvert	vous	**ouvrissiez**
ils	**ont** ouvert	ils	**ouvrissent**

CONSTRUCTIONS

ouvrir une porte toute grande   to open a door wide
ouvrir l'électricité/le gaz/la radio   to switch or turn on
the electricity/gas/radio
notre épicier ouvre le lundi   our grocer is open on
Mondays
s'ouvrir   to open; to open up; to open out

67 paraître

to appear   *also* **disparaître**
to disappear

PRESENT PARTICIPLE
paraissant

PAST PARTICIPLE
paru

PRESENT
je	**parais**
tu	**parais**
il	**paraît**
nous	**paraissons**
vous	**paraissez**
ils	**paraissent**

IMPERFECT
je	**paraissais**
tu	**paraissais**
il	**paraissait**
nous	**paraissions**
vous	**paraissiez**
ils	**paraissaient**

FUTURE
je	**paraîtrai**
tu	**paraîtras**
il	**paraîtra**
nous	**paraîtrons**
vous	**paraîtrez**
ils	**paraîtront**

IMPERATIVE
parais
paraissons
paraissez

CONDITIONAL
je	**paraîtrais**
tu	**paraîtrais**
il	**paraîtrait**
nous	**paraîtrions**
vous	**paraîtriez**
ils	**paraîtraient**

PAST HISTORIC		PRESENT SUBJUNCTIVE	
je	**par**us	je	**par**aisse
tu	**par**us	tu	**par**aisses
il	**par**ut	il	**par**aisse
nous	**par**ûmes	nous	**par**aissions
vous	**par**ûtes	vous	**par**aissiez
ils	**par**urent	ils	**par**aissent

PERFECT		PAST SUBJUNCTIVE	
j'	**ai** paru	je	**par**usse
tu	**as** paru	tu	**par**usses
il	**a** paru	il	**par**ût
nous	**avons** paru	nous	**par**ussions
vous	**avez** paru	vous	**par**ussiez
ils	**ont** paru	ils	**par**ussent

CONSTRUCTIONS

paraître faire qch   to seem to do sth
'vient de paraître'   'just out'
'à paraître prochainement'   'out soon'
il est malade, paraît-il,   il paraît qu'il est malade   he's ill
apparently

68 partir
to go, leave

PRESENT PARTICIPLE
partant

PAST PARTICIPLE
parti

PRESENT		IMPERFECT	
je	**pars**	je	**part**ais
tu	**pars**	tu	**part**ais
il	**part**	il	**part**ait
nous	**part**ons	nous	**part**ions
vous	**part**ez	vous	**part**iez
ils	**part**ent	ils	**part**aient

		FUTURE	
		je	**part**irai
		tu	**part**iras
		il	**part**ira
		nous	**part**irons
		vous	**part**irez
		ils	**part**iront

IMPERATIVE	CONDITIONAL	
pars	je	**part**irais
partons	tu	**part**irais
partez	il	**part**irait
	nous	**part**irions
	vous	**part**iriez
	ils	**part**iraient

PAST HISTORIC		PRESENT SUBJUNCTIVE	
je	**part**is	je	**part**e
tu	**part**is	tu	**part**es
il	**part**it	il	**part**e
nous	**part**îmes	nous	**part**ions
vous	**part**îtes	vous	**part**iez
ils	**part**irent	ils	**part**ent

PERFECT		PAST SUBJUNCTIVE	
je	suis **part**i	je	**part**isse
tu	es **part**i	tu	**part**isses
il	est **part**i	il	**part**ît
nous	sommes **part**is	nous	**part**issions
vous	êtes **part**i(s)	vous	**part**issiez
ils	sont **part**is	ils	**part**issent

CONSTRUCTIONS

partir en vacances/en voyage   to go (off) on holiday/on a journey
à partir du 14 juillet   as from the 14th of July
à partir de 100 F   from 100 F upwards

69 passer

to pass

also dépasser
to overtake

PRESENT PARTICIPLE
passant

surpasser
to surpass

PAST PARTICIPLE
passé

PRESENT		*IMPERFECT*	
je	**passe**	je	**passais**
tu	**passes**	tu	**passais**
il	**passe**	il	**passait**
nous	**passons**	nous	**passions**
vous	**passez**	vous	**passiez**
ils	**passent**	ils	**passaient**

		FUTURE	
		je	**passerai**
		tu	**passeras**
		il	**passera**
		nous	**passerons**
		vous	**passerez**
		ils	**passeront**

IMPERATIVE	*CONDITIONAL*	
passe	je	**passerais**
passons	tu	**passerais**
passez	il	**passerait**
	nous	**passerions**
	vous	**passeriez**
	ils	**passeraient**

PAST HISTORIC		PRESENT SUBJUNCTIVE	
je	**pass**ai	je	**pass**e
tu	**pass**as	tu	**pass**es
il	**pass**a	il	**pass**e
nous	**pass**âmes	nous	**pass**ions
vous	**pass**âtes	vous	**pass**iez
ils	**pass**èrent	ils	**pass**ent

PERFECT		PAST SUBJUNCTIVE	
j'	**ai passé**	je	**pass**asse
tu	**as passé**	tu	**pass**asses
il	**a passé**	il	**pass**ât
nous	**avons passé**	nous	**pass**assions
vous	**avez passé**	vous	**pass**assiez
ils	**ont passé**	ils	**pass**assent

CONSTRUCTIONS

passer en courant   to run past
passer au bureau/chez un ami   to call (in) at the office/at a friend's
laisser passer qn   to let sb through *or* in *etc*
laisser passer une erreur   to overlook a mistake
passer un examen   to sit an exam

70 payer

to pay

also **balayer**
to sweep up

PRESENT PARTICIPLE
payant

débrayer
to declutch

PAST PARTICIPLE
payé

délayer
to thin down

PRESENT

je	**paye**
tu	**payes**
il	**paye**
nous	**payons**
vous	**payez**
ils	**payent**

IMPERFECT

je	**payais**
tu	**payais**
il	**payait**
nous	**payions**
vous	**payiez**
ils	**payaient**

FUTURE

je	**payerai**
tu	**payeras**
il	**payera**
nous	**payerons**
vous	**payerez**
ils	**payeront**

IMPERATIVE

paye
payons
payez

CONDITIONAL

je	**payerais**
tu	**payerais**
il	**payerait**
nous	**payerions**
vous	**payeriez**
ils	**payeraient**

to pay

effrayer
to frighten

essayer
to try

PAST HISTORIC		*PRESENT SUBJUNCTIVE*	
je	**payai**	je	**paye**
tu	**payas**	tu	**payes**
il	**paya**	il	**paye**
nous	**payâmes**	nous	**payions**
vous	**payâtes**	vous	**payiez**
ils	**payèrent**	ils	**payent**
PERFECT		*PAST SUBJUNCTIVE*	
j'	**ai payé**	je	**payasse**
tu	**as payé**	tu	**payasses**
il	**a payé**	il	**payât**
nous	**avons payé**	nous	**payassions**
vous	**avez payé**	vous	**payassiez**
ils	**ont payé**	ils	**payassent**

CONSTRUCTIONS
être payé par chèque/à l'heure to be paid by cheque/by the hour
est-ce qu'il t'a payé les billets? did he pay you for the tickets?
il l'a payé 10 F he paid 10 F for it
il l'a payé de sa vie it cost him his life

71 peindre
to paint

also **atteindre**
to reach

PRESENT PARTICIPLE
peignant

déteindre
to lose its colour

PAST PARTICIPLE
peint

enfreindre
to infringe

PRESENT
je	peins
tu	peins
il	peint
nous	peignons
vous	peignez
ils	peignent

IMPERFECT
je	peignais
tu	peignais
il	peignait
nous	peignions
vous	peigniez
ils	peignaient

FUTURE
je	**peind**rai
tu	**peind**ras
il	**peind**ra
nous	**peind**rons
vous	**peind**rez
ils	**peind**ront

IMPERATIVE
peins
peignons
peignez

CONDITIONAL
je	**peind**rais
tu	**peind**rais
il	**peind**rait
nous	**peind**rions
vous	**peind**riez
ils	**peind**raient

154

peindre 71
to paint

éteindre
  to put out

teindre
  to dye

PAST HISTORIC		PRESENT SUBJUNCTIVE	
je	peignis	je	peigne
tu	peignis	tu	peignes
il	peignit	il	peigne
nous	peignîmes	nous	peignions
vous	peignîtes	vous	peigniez
ils	peignirent	ils	peignent

PERFECT		PAST SUBJUNCTIVE	
j'	**ai** peint	je	peignisse
tu	**as** peint	tu	peignisses
il	**a** peint	il	peignît
nous	**avons** peint	nous	peignissions
vous	**avez** peint	vous	peignissiez
ils	**ont** peint	ils	peignissent

CONSTRUCTIONS
peindre qch en bleu/à l'huile   to paint sth blue/in oils

72 perdre
to lose

PRESENT PARTICIPLE
perdant

PAST PARTICIPLE
perdu

PRESENT

je	**perds**
tu	**perds**
il	**perd**
nous	**perd**ons
vous	**perd**ez
ils	**perd**ent

IMPERFECT

je	**perd**ais
tu	**perd**ais
il	**perd**ait
nous	**perd**ions
vous	**perd**iez
ils	**perd**aient

FUTURE

je	**perd**rai
tu	**perd**ras
il	**perd**ra
nous	**perd**rons
vous	**perd**rez
ils	**perd**ront

IMPERATIVE

perds
perdons
perdez

CONDITIONAL

je	**perd**rais
tu	**perd**rais
il	**perd**rait
nous	**perd**rions
vous	**perd**riez
ils	**perd**raient

PAST HISTORIC		PRESENT SUBJUNCTIVE	
je	**perd**is	je	**perd**e
tu	**perd**is	tu	**perd**es
il	**perd**it	il	**perd**e
nous	**perd**îmes	nous	**perd**ions
vous	**perd**îtes	vous	**perd**iez
ils	**perd**irent	ils	**perd**ent

PERFECT		PAST SUBJUNCTIVE	
j'	**ai perd**u	je	**perd**isse
tu	**as perd**u	tu	**perd**isses
il	**a perd**u	il	**perd**ît
nous	**avons perd**u	nous	**perd**issions
vous	**avez perd**u	vous	**perd**issiez
ils	**ont perd**u	ils	**perd**issent

CONSTRUCTIONS

perdre qn/qch de vue to lose sight of sb/sth
perdre espoir/connaissance/du poids to lose
hope/consciousness/weight
tu perds ton temps à essayer you're wasting your time
trying
se perdre to get lost; to disappear

73 permettre
to allow

PRESENT PARTICIPLE
permettant

PAST PARTICIPLE
permis

PRESENT		*IMPERFECT*	
je	permets	je	**permettais**
tu	permets	tu	**permettais**
il	permet	il	**permettait**
nous	**permettons**	nous	**permettions**
vous	**permettez**	vous	**permettiez**
ils	**permettent**	ils	**permettaient**

		FUTURE	
		je	**permettrai**
		tu	**permettras**
		il	**permettra**
		nous	**permettrons**
		vous	**permettrez**
		ils	**permettront**

IMPERATIVE	*CONDITIONAL*	
permets	je	**permettrais**
permettons	tu	**permettrais**
permettez	il	**permettrait**
	nous	**permettrions**
	vous	**permettriez**
	ils	**permettraient**

PAST HISTORIC		PRESENT SUBJUNCTIVE	
je	permis	je	**permette**
tu	permis	tu	**permettes**
il	permit	il	**permette**
nous	permîmes	nous	**permettions**
vous	permîtes	vous	**permettiez**
ils	permirent	ils	**permettent**

PERFECT		PAST SUBJUNCTIVE	
j'	**ai** permis	je	permisse
tu	**as** permis	tu	permisses
il	**a** permis	il	permît
nous	**avons** permis	nous	permissions
vous	**avez** permis	vous	permissiez
ils	**ont** permis	ils	permissent

CONSTRUCTIONS

permettre à qn de faire qch   to allow sb to do sth
permettre qch à qn   to allow sb sth
mes moyens ne me le permettent pas   I can't afford it
permettez-moi de vous présenter ma sœur   may I
introduce my sister?

74 plaire

to please   *also* **déplaire**
                     to displease

PRESENT PARTICIPLE
plaisant

PAST PARTICIPLE
plu

PRESENT		*IMPERFECT*	
je	**plais**	je	**plaisais**
tu	**plais**	tu	**plaisais**
il	**plaît**	il	**plaisait**
nous	**plaisons**	nous	**plaisions**
vous	**plaisez**	vous	**plaisiez**
ils	**plaisent**	ils	**plaisaient**

		FUTURE	
		je	**plairai**
		tu	**plairas**
		il	**plaira**
		nous	**plairons**
		vous	**plairez**
		ils	**plairont**

IMPERATIVE		*CONDITIONAL*	
	plais	je	**plairais**
	plaisons	tu	**plairais**
	plaisez	il	**plairait**
		nous	**plairions**
		vous	**plairiez**
		ils	**plairaient**

PAST HISTORIC		PRESENT SUBJUNCTIVE	
je	**plus**	je	**plaise**
tu	**plus**	tu	**plaises**
il	**plut**	il	**plaise**
nous	**plûmes**	nous	**plaisions**
vous	**plûtes**	vous	**plaisiez**
ils	**plurent**	ils	**plaisent**

PERFECT		PAST SUBJUNCTIVE	
j'	**ai** plu	je	**plusse**
tu	**as** plu	tu	**plusses**
il	**a** plu	il	**plût**
nous	**avons** plu	nous	**plussions**
vous	**avez** plu	vous	**plussiez**
ils	**ont** plu	ils	**plussent**

CONSTRUCTIONS

sa maison lui plaît   she likes her house
il cherche à plaire à tout le monde   he tries to please
everybody
j'irai si ça me plaît   I'll go if I feel like it
s'il te plaît, s'il vous plaît   please
il se plaît à Paris   he likes being in Paris

75 pleuvoir
to rain

PRESENT PARTICIPLE
pleuvant

PAST PARTICIPLE
plu

PRESENT	*IMPERFECT*
il pleut	**il pleuvait**

	FUTURE
	il pleuvra

IMPERATIVE	*CONDITIONAL*
not used	**il pleuvrait**

to rain

PAST HISTORIC
il plut

PRESENT SUBJUNCTIVE
il pleuve

PERFECT
il a plu

PAST SUBJUNCTIVE
il plût

CONSTRUCTIONS
il pleut it's raining
il pleut à verse it's pouring

76 pourvoir
to provide

PRESENT PARTICIPLE
pourvoyant

PAST PARTICIPLE
pourvu

PRESENT		*IMPERFECT*	
je	**pourv**ois	je	**pourv**oyais
tu	**pourv**ois	tu	**pourv**oyais
il	**pourv**oit	il	**pourv**oyait
nous	**pourv**oyons	nous	**pourv**oyions
vous	**pourv**oyez	vous	**pourv**oyiez
ils	**pourv**oient	ils	**pourv**oyaient

		FUTURE	
		je	**pourv**oirai
		tu	**pourv**oiras
		il	**pourv**oira
		nous	**pourv**oirons
		vous	**pourv**oirez
		ils	**pourv**oiront

IMPERATIVE	*CONDITIONAL*	
pourvois	je	**pourv**oirais
pourvoyons	tu	**pourv**oirais
pourvoyez	il	**pourv**oirait
	nous	**pourv**oirions
	vous	**pourv**oiriez
	ils	**pourv**oiraient

to provide

PAST HISTORIC

je	**pourvus**
tu	**pourvus**
il	**pourvut**
nous	**pourvûmes**
vous	**pourvûtes**
ils	**pourvurent**

PRESENT SUBJUNCTIVE

je	**pourvoie**
tu	**pourvoies**
il	**pourvoie**
nous	**pourvoyions**
vous	**pourvoyiez**
ils	**pourvoient**

PERFECT

j'	**ai pourvu**
tu	**as pourvu**
il	**a pourvu**
nous	**avons pourvu**
vous	**avez pourvu**
ils	**ont pourvu**

PAST SUBJUNCTIVE

je	**pourvusse**
tu	**pourvusses**
il	**pourvût**
nous	**pourvussions**
vous	**pourvussiez**
ils	**pourvussent**

CONSTRUCTIONS

pourvoir qch de qch to equip sth with sth
pourvoir aux besoins de qn to provide for sb's needs

77 pouvoir
to be able

PRESENT PARTICIPLE
pouvant

PAST PARTICIPLE
pu

PRESENT		*IMPERFECT*	
je	**peux**	je	**pouv**ais
tu	**peux**	tu	**pouv**ais
il	**peut**	il	**pouv**ait
nous	**pouv**ons	nous	**pouv**ions
vous	**pouv**ez	vous	**pouv**iez
ils	**peuv**ent	ils	**pouv**aient

		FUTURE	
		je	**pourr**ai
		tu	**pourr**as
		il	**pourr**a
		nous	**pourr**ons
		vous	**pourr**ez
		ils	**pourr**ont

IMPERATIVE		*CONDITIONAL*	
	not used	je	**pourr**ais
		tu	**pourr**ais
		il	**pourr**ait
		nous	**pourr**ions
		vous	**pourr**iez
		ils	**pourr**aient

PAST HISTORIC		PRESENT SUBJUNCTIVE	
je	pus	je	puisse
tu	pus	tu	puisses
il	put	il	puisse
nous	pûmes	nous	puissions
vous	pûtes	vous	puissiez
ils	purent	ils	puissent

PERFECT		PAST SUBJUNCTIVE	
j'	**ai** pu	je	pusse
tu	**as** pu	tu	pusses
il	**a** pu	il	pût
nous	**avons** pu	nous	pussions
vous	**avez** pu	vous	pussiez
ils	**ont** pu	ils	pussent

CONSTRUCTIONS

pouvoir faire to be able to do
il ne peut pas venir he can't come
il n'en peut plus he's tired out; he's had enough
il a été on ne peut plus aimable he couldn't have been
kinder

78 prendre

to take

also **entreprendre**
to undertake

PRESENT PARTICIPLE
prenant

se méprendre
to be mistaken

PAST PARTICIPLE
pris

surprendre
to surprise

PRESENT
je	**prends**
tu	**prends**
il	**prend**
nous	prenons
vous	prenez
ils	prennent

IMPERFECT
je	prenais
tu	prenais
il	prenait
nous	prenions
vous	preniez
ils	prenaient

FUTURE
je	**prendrai**
tu	**prendras**
il	**prendra**
nous	**prendrons**
vous	**prendrez**
ils	**prendront**

IMPERATIVE
prends
prenons
prenez

CONDITIONAL
je	**prendrais**
tu	**prendrais**
il	**prendrait**
nous	**prendrions**
vous	**prendriez**
ils	**prendraient**

PAST HISTORIC		PRESENT SUBJUNCTIVE	
je	pris	je	prenne
tu	pris	tu	prennes
il	prit	il	prenne
nous	prîmes	nous	prenions
vous	prîtes	vous	preniez
ils	prirent	ils	prennent

PERFECT		PAST SUBJUNCTIVE	
j'	ai pris	je	prisse
tu	as pris	tu	prisses
il	a pris	il	prît
nous	avons pris	nous	prissions
vous	avez pris	vous	prissiez
ils	ont pris	ils	prissent

CONSTRUCTIONS

prendre qch à qn   to take sth from sb
il l'a pris dans un tiroir/sur la table   he took it out of a drawer/from the table
prendre feu   to catch fire
prendre qn en amitié/en aversion   to take a liking/a dislike to sb

79 promettre
to promise

also **compromettre**
to compromise

PRESENT PARTICIPLE
promettant

PAST PARTICIPLE
promis

PRESENT		*IMPERFECT*	
je	**promets**	je	**promett**ais
tu	**promets**	tu	**promett**ais
il	**promet**	il	**promett**ait
nous	**promett**ons	nous	**promett**ions
vous	**promett**ez	vous	**promett**iez
ils	**promett**ent	ils	**promett**aient

		FUTURE	
		je	**promett**rai
		tu	**promett**ras
		il	**promett**ra
		nous	**promett**rons
		vous	**promett**rez
		ils	**promett**ront

IMPERATIVE	*CONDITIONAL*	
promets	je	**promett**rais
promettons	tu	**promett**rais
promettez	il	**promett**rait
	nous	**promett**rions
	vous	**promett**riez
	ils	**promett**raient

PAST HISTORIC		*PRESENT SUBJUNCTIVE*	
je	promis	je	**promette**
tu	promis	tu	**promettes**
il	promit	il	**promette**
nous	promîmes	nous	**promettions**
vous	promîtes	vous	**promettiez**
ils	promirent	ils	**promettent**
PERFECT		*PAST SUBJUNCTIVE*	
j'	**ai** promis	je	promisse
tu	**as** promis	tu	promisses
il	**a** promis	il	promît
nous	**avons** promis	nous	promissions
vous	**avez** promis	vous	promissiez
ils	**ont** promis	ils	promissent

CONSTRUCTIONS

promettre qch à qn   to promise sth to sb
promettre à qn de faire qch   to promise sb that one will do sth
on nous promet du beau temps   we're in for some fine weather, they say
se promettre de faire   to resolve to do

80 protéger
to protect

also **abréger**
to shorten

PRESENT PARTICIPLE
protégeant

alléger
to lighten

PAST PARTICIPLE
protégé

assiéger
to besiege

PRESENT			*IMPERFECT*	
je	protège		je	protégeais
tu	protèges		tu	protégeais
il	protège		il	protégeait
nous	protégeons		nous	protégions
vous	protégez		vous	protégiez
ils	protègent		ils	protégeaient

FUTURE

je	protégerai
tu	protégeras
il	protégera
nous	protégerons
vous	protégerez
ils	protégeront

IMPERATIVE		*CONDITIONAL*	
	protège	je	protégerais
	protégeons	tu	protégerais
	protégez	il	protégerait
		nous	protégerions
		vous	protégeriez
		ils	protégeraient

piéger
to booby-trap

PAST HISTORIC

je	**protég**eai
tu	**protég**eas
il	**protég**ea
nous	**protég**eâmes
vous	**protég**eâtes
ils	**protég**èrent

PRESENT SUBJUNCTIVE

je	**protèg**e
tu	**protèg**es
il	**protèg**e
nous	**protég**ions
vous	**protég**iez
ils	**protèg**ent

PERFECT

j'	**ai prot**égé
tu	**as prot**égé
il	**a prot**égé
nous	**avons prot**égé
vous	**avez prot**égé
ils	**ont prot**égé

PAST SUBJUNCTIVE

je	**protég**easse
tu	**protég**easses
il	**protég**eât
nous	**protég**eassions
vous	**protég**eassiez
ils	**protég**eassent

CONSTRUCTIONS
se protéger de qch/contre qch   to protect oneself from sth/against sth

81 recevoir

to receive   *also*   **apercevoir**
                                 to see

PRESENT PARTICIPLE
recevant

                            décevoir
                            to disappoint

PAST PARTICIPLE
reçu

                            percevoir
                            to perceive

PRESENT

je	**reç**ois
tu	**reç**ois
il	**reç**oit
nous	**recev**ons
vous	**recev**ez
ils	**reç**oivent

IMPERFECT

je	**recev**ais
tu	**recev**ais
il	**recev**ait
nous	**recev**ions
vous	**recev**iez
ils	**recev**aient

FUTURE

je	**recev**rai
tu	**recev**ras
il	**recev**ra
nous	**recev**rons
vous	**recev**rez
ils	**recev**ront

IMPERATIVE

reçois
recevons
recevez

CONDITIONAL

je	**recev**rais
tu	**recev**rais
il	**recev**rait
nous	**recev**rions
vous	**recev**riez
ils	**recev**raient

PAST HISTORIC

je	reçus
tu	reçus
il	reçut
nous	reçûmes
vous	reçûtes
ils	reçurent

PRESENT SUBJUNCTIVE

je	reçoive
tu	reçoives
il	reçoive
nous	**recev**ions
vous	**recev**iez
ils	reçoivent

PERFECT

j'	**ai** reçu
tu	**as** reçu
il	**a** reçu
nous	**avons** reçu
vous	**avez** reçu
ils	**ont** reçu

PAST SUBJUNCTIVE

je	reçusse
tu	reçusses
il	reçût
nous	reçussions
vous	reçussiez
ils	reçussent

CONSTRUCTIONS

recevoir un cadeau de qn   to receive a present from sb
être reçu à un examen   to pass an exam
être reçu à l'université   to get a place at university
il a reçu un coup de pied   he got kicked

82 rendre
to give back

PRESENT PARTICIPLE
rendant

PAST PARTICIPLE
rendu

PRESENT		IMPERFECT	
je	**rend**s	je	**rend**ais
tu	**rend**s	tu	**rend**ais
il	**rend**	il	**rend**ait
nous	**rend**ons	nous	**rend**ions
vous	**rend**ez	vous	**rend**iez
ils	**rend**ent	ils	**rend**aient

		FUTURE	
		je	**rend**rai
		tu	**rend**ras
		il	**rend**ra
		nous	**rend**rons
		vous	**rend**rez
		ils	**rend**ront

IMPERATIVE	CONDITIONAL	
rends	je	**rend**rais
rendons	tu	**rend**rais
rendez	il	**rend**rait
	nous	**rend**rions
	vous	**rend**riez
	ils	**rend**raient

PAST HISTORIC		PRESENT SUBJUNCTIVE	
je	rendis	je	rende
tu	rendis	tu	rendes
il	rendit	il	rende
nous	rendîmes	nous	rendions
vous	rendîtes	vous	rendiez
ils	rendirent	ils	rendent

PERFECT		PAST SUBJUNCTIVE	
j'	ai rendu	je	rendisse
tu	as rendu	tu	rendisses
il	a rendu	il	rendît
nous	avons rendu	nous	rendissions
vous	avez rendu	vous	rendissiez
ils	ont rendu	ils	rendissent

CONSTRUCTIONS

rendre qch à qn   to give sth back to sb
rendre qn heureux   to make sb happy
rendre visite à qn   to pay sb a visit
se rendre   to surrender
se rendre compte de qch   to realize sth

83 rentrer
to go back; to go in

PRESENT PARTICIPLE
rentrant

PAST PARTICIPLE
rentré

PRESENT		*IMPERFECT*	
je	**rentr**e	je	**rentr**ais
tu	**rentr**es	tu	**rentr**ais
il	**rentr**e	il	**rentr**ait
nous	**rentr**ons	nous	**rentr**ions
vous	**rentr**ez	vous	**rentr**iez
ils	**rentr**ent	ils	**rentr**aient

		FUTURE	
		je	**rentr**erai
		tu	**rentr**eras
		il	**rentr**era
		nous	**rentr**erons
		vous	**rentr**erez
		ils	**rentr**eront

IMPERATIVE	*CONDITIONAL*	
rentre	je	**rentr**erais
rentrons	tu	**rentr**erais
rentrez	il	**rentr**erait
	nous	**rentr**erions
	vous	**rentr**eriez
	ils	**rentr**eraient

to go back; to go in

PAST HISTORIC		PRESENT SUBJUNCTIVE	
je	**rentrai**	je	**rentre**
tu	**rentras**	tu	**rentres**
il	**rentra**	il	**rentre**
nous	**rentrâmes**	nous	**rentrions**
vous	**rentrâtes**	vous	**rentriez**
ils	**rentrèrent**	ils	**rentrent**

PERFECT		PAST SUBJUNCTIVE	
je	**suis rentré**	je	**rentrasse**
tu	**es rentré**	tu	**rentrasses**
il	**est rentré**	il	**rentrât**
nous	**sommes rentrés**	nous	**rentrassions**
vous	**êtes rentré(s)**	vous	**rentrassiez**
ils	**sont rentrés**	ils	**rentrassent**

CONSTRUCTIONS

rentrer à la maison to go back home
rentrer dans une firme to join a firm
rentrer dans un arbre to crash into a tree
il a rentré la voiture he put the car away
rentrer ses griffes to draw in one's claws

84 répondre

to answer

also **confondre**
to confuse

PRESENT PARTICIPLE
répondant

correspondre
to correspond

PAST PARTICIPLE
répondu

tondre
to shear

PRESENT

je	**réponds**
tu	**réponds**
il	**répond**
nous	**répondons**
vous	**répondez**
ils	**répondent**

IMPERFECT

je	**répondais**
tu	**répondais**
il	**répondait**
nous	**répondions**
vous	**répondiez**
ils	**répondaient**

FUTURE

je	**répondrai**
tu	**répondras**
il	**répondra**
nous	**répondrons**
vous	**répondrez**
ils	**répondront**

IMPERATIVE

réponds
répondons
répondez

CONDITIONAL

je	**répondrais**
tu	**répondrais**
il	**répondrait**
nous	**répondrions**
vous	**répondriez**
ils	**répondraient**

PAST HISTORIC		*PRESENT SUBJUNCTIVE*	
je	**répond**is	je	**répond**e
tu	**répond**is	tu	**répond**es
il	**répond**it	il	**répond**e
nous	**répond**îmes	nous	**répond**ions
vous	**répond**îtes	vous	**répond**iez
ils	**répond**irent	ils	**répond**ent
PERFECT		*PAST SUBJUNCTIVE*	
j'	**ai répond**u	je	**répond**isse
tu	**as répond**u	tu	**répond**isses
il	**a répond**u	il	**répond**ît
nous	**avons répond**u	nous	**répond**issions
vous	**avez répond**u	vous	**répond**issiez
ils	**ont répond**u	ils	**répond**issent

CONSTRUCTIONS

répondre à qn/à une question to answer sb/a question
on a sonné – va répondre that's the bell – go and answer the door
ça ne répond pas there's no reply
répondre de qn to answer for sb

85 résoudre
to solve

PRESENT PARTICIPLE
résolvant

PAST PARTICIPLE
résolu

PRESENT		*IMPERFECT*	
je	**résous**	je	**résolvais**
tu	**résous**	tu	**résolvais**
il	**résout**	il	**résolvait**
nous	**résolvons**	nous	**résolvions**
vous	**résolvez**	vous	**résolviez**
ils	**résolvent**	ils	**résolvaient**

		FUTURE	
		je	**résoudrai**
		tu	**résoudras**
		il	**résoudra**
		nous	**résoudrons**
		vous	**résoudrez**
		ils	**résoudront**

IMPERATIVE		*CONDITIONAL*	
	résous	je	**résoudrais**
	résolvons	tu	**résoudrais**
	résolvez	il	**résoudrait**
		nous	**résoudrions**
		vous	**résoudriez**
		ils	**résoudraient**

182

PAST HISTORIC		PRESENT SUBJUNCTIVE	
je	résolus	je	résolve
tu	résolus	tu	résolves
il	résolut	il	résolve
nous	résolûmes	nous	résolvions
vous	résolûtes	vous	résolviez
ils	résolurent	ils	résolvent

PERFECT		PAST SUBJUNCTIVE	
j'	**ai** résolu	je	résolusse
tu	**as** résolu	tu	résolusses
il	**a** résolu	il	résolût
nous	**avons** résolu	nous	résolussions
vous	**avez** résolu	vous	résolussiez
ils	**ont** résolu	ils	résolussent

CONSTRUCTIONS

se résoudre à faire qch   to resolve to do sth
être résolu à faire   to be set on doing

86 rester
to remain

PRESENT PARTICIPLE
restant

PAST PARTICIPLE
resté

PRESENT		*IMPERFECT*	
je	**rest**e	je	**rest**ais
tu	**rest**es	tu	**rest**ais
il	**rest**e	il	**rest**ait
nous	**rest**ons	nous	**rest**ions
vous	**rest**ez	vous	**rest**iez
ils	**rest**ent	ils	**rest**aient

		FUTURE	
		je	**rest**erai
		tu	**rest**eras
		il	**rest**era
		nous	**rest**erons
		vous	**rest**erez
		ils	**rest**eront

IMPERATIVE		*CONDITIONAL*	
	reste	je	**rest**erais
	restons	tu	**rest**erais
	restez	il	**rest**erait
		nous	**rest**erions
		vous	**rest**eriez
		ils	**rest**eraient

PAST HISTORIC		PRESENT SUBJUNCTIVE	
je	restai	je	reste
tu	restas	tu	restes
il	resta	il	reste
nous	restâmes	nous	restions
vous	restâtes	vous	restiez
ils	restèrent	ils	restent

PERFECT		PAST SUBJUNCTIVE	
je	suis resté	je	restasse
tu	es resté	tu	restasses
il	est resté	il	restât
nous	sommes restés	nous	restassions
vous	êtes resté(s)	vous	restassiez
ils	sont restés	ils	restassent

CONSTRUCTIONS
il est resté à regarder la télévision he stayed watching television
c'est tout l'argent qui leur reste that's all the money they have left
il reste encore un peu de pain there's still a little bread left

87 retourner
to return

PRESENT PARTICIPLE
retournant

PAST PARTICIPLE
retourné

PRESENT

je	**retourne**
tu	**retournes**
il	**retourne**
nous	**retournons**
vous	**retournez**
ils	**retournent**

IMPERFECT

je	**retournais**
tu	**retournais**
il	**retournait**
nous	**retournions**
vous	**retourniez**
ils	**retournaient**

FUTURE

je	**retournerai**
tu	**retourneras**
il	**retournera**
nous	**retournerons**
vous	**retournerez**
ils	**retourneront**

IMPERATIVE

retourne
retournons
retournez

CONDITIONAL

je	**retournerais**
tu	**retournerais**
il	**retournerait**
nous	**retournerions**
vous	**retourneriez**
ils	**retourneraient**

to return

PAST HISTORIC		PRESENT SUBJUNCTIVE	
je	**retourn**ai	je	**retourn**e
tu	**retourn**as	tu	**retourn**es
il	**retourn**a	il	**retourn**e
nous	**retourn**âmes	nous	**retourn**ions
vous	**retourn**âtes	vous	**retourn**iez
ils	**retourn**èrent	ils	**retourn**ent

PERFECT		PAST SUBJUNCTIVE	
je	suis **retourn**é	je	**retourn**asse
tu	es **retourn**é	tu	**retourn**asses
il	est **retourn**é	il	**retourn**ât
nous	sommes	nous	**retourn**assions
	retournés	vous	**retourn**assiez
vous	êtes **retourn**é(s)	ils	**retourn**assent
ils	sont **retourn**és		

CONSTRUCTIONS

il a retourné le seau/sac he turned the bucket upside down/the bag inside out

il a retourné les marchandises he sent the goods back

retourner en Italie to go back to Italy

se retourner to turn over; to turn round

88 revenir
to come back

PRESENT PARTICIPLE
revenant

PAST PARTICIPLE
revenu

PRESENT		*IMPERFECT*	
je	**reviens**	je	**revenais**
tu	**reviens**	tu	**revenais**
il	**revient**	il	**revenait**
nous	**revenons**	nous	**revenions**
vous	**revenez**	vous	**reveniez**
ils	**reviennent**	ils	**revenaient**

		FUTURE	
		je	**reviendrai**
		tu	**reviendras**
		il	**reviendra**
		nous	**reviendrons**
		vous	**reviendrez**
		ils	**reviendront**

IMPERATIVE		*CONDITIONAL*	
	reviens	je	**reviendrais**
	revenons	tu	**reviendrais**
	revenez	il	**reviendrait**
		nous	**reviendrions**
		vous	**reviendriez**
		ils	**reviendraient**

PAST HISTORIC		PRESENT SUBJUNCTIVE	
je	revins	je	revienne
tu	revins	tu	reviennes
il	revint	il	revienne
nous	revînmes	nous	revenions
vous	revîntes	vous	reveniez
ils	revinrent	ils	reviennent

PERFECT		PAST SUBJUNCTIVE	
je	suis revenu	je	revinsse
tu	es revenu	tu	revinsses
il	est revenu	il	revînt
nous	sommes revenus	nous	revinssions
vous	êtes revenu(s)	vous	revinssiez
ils	sont revenus	ils	revinssent

CONSTRUCTIONS

le repas revient à 70 F   the meal comes to 70 F
il est revenu à Paris   he came back to Paris
il est revenu de Paris   he's back from Paris
revenir sur une promesse   to go back on a promise
revenir sur ses pas   to retrace one's steps

89 rire

to laugh

also **sourire**
to smile

PRESENT PARTICIPLE
riant

PAST PARTICIPLE
ri

PRESENT

je **ris**
tu **ris**
il **rit**
nous **rions**
vous **riez**
ils **rient**

IMPERFECT

je **riais**
tu **riais**
il **riait**
nous **riions**
vous **riiez**
ils **riaient**

FUTURE

je **rirai**
tu **riras**
il **rira**
nous **rirons**
vous **rirez**
ils **riront**

IMPERATIVE

ris
rions
riez

CONDITIONAL

je **rirais**
tu **rirais**
il **rirait**
nous **ririons**
vous **ririez**
ils **riraient**

PAST HISTORIC

je	**ris**
tu	**ris**
il	**rit**
nous	**rîmes**
vous	**rîtes**
ils	**rirent**

PERFECT

j'	**ai**	ri
tu	**as**	ri
il	**a**	ri
nous	**avons**	ri
vous	**avez**	ri
ils	**ont**	ri

PRESENT SUBJUNCTIVE

je	**rie**
tu	**ries**
il	**rie**
nous	**riions**
vous	**riiez**
ils	**rient**

PAST SUBJUNCTIVE

je	**risse**
tu	**risses**
il	**rît**
nous	**rissions**
vous	**rissiez**
ils	**rissent**

CONSTRUCTIONS

rire de qn/qch to laugh at sb/sth
il a fait cela pour rire he did it for a joke
rire aux éclats to roar with laughter

90 rompre

to break

also **corrompre**
to corrupt

interrompre
to interrupt

PRESENT PARTICIPLE
rompant

PAST PARTICIPLE
rompu

PRESENT

je	**romps**
tu	**romps**
il	**rompt**
nous	**rompons**
vous	**rompez**
ils	**rompent**

IMPERFECT

je	**rompais**
tu	**rompais**
il	**rompait**
nous	**rompions**
vous	**rompiez**
ils	**rompaient**

FUTURE

je	**romprai**
tu	**rompras**
il	**rompra**
nous	**romprons**
vous	**romprez**
ils	**rompront**

IMPERATIVE

romps
rompons
rompez

CONDITIONAL

je	**romprais**
tu	**romprais**
il	**romprait**
nous	**romprions**
vous	**rompriez**
ils	**rompraient**

rompre **90**
to break

PAST HISTORIC		PRESENT SUBJUNCTIVE	
je	rompis	je	rompe
tu	rompis	tu	rompes
il	rompit	il	rompe
nous	rompîmes	nous	rompions
vous	rompîtes	vous	rompiez
ils	rompirent	ils	rompent

PERFECT		PAST SUBJUNCTIVE	
j'	ai rompu	je	rompisse
tu	as rompu	tu	rompisses
il	a rompu	il	rompît
nous	avons rompu	nous	rompissions
vous	avez rompu	vous	rompissiez
ils	ont rompu	ils	rompissent

CONSTRUCTIONS
ils ont rompu (leurs fiançailles) they've broken off their engagement
rompre les rangs to fall out
se rompre to break; to burst
être rompu (de fatigue) to be exhausted

91 savoir
to know

PRESENT PARTICIPLE
sachant

PAST PARTICIPLE
su

PRESENT		*IMPERFECT*	
je	**sais**	je	**savais**
tu	**sais**	tu	**savais**
il	**sait**	il	**savait**
nous	**savons**	nous	**savions**
vous	**savez**	vous	**saviez**
ils	**savent**	ils	**savaient**

		FUTURE	
		je	**saurai**
		tu	**sauras**
		il	**saura**
		nous	**saurons**
		vous	**saurez**
		ils	**sauront**

IMPERATIVE		*CONDITIONAL*	
	sache	je	**saurais**
	sachons	tu	**saurais**
	sachez	il	**saurait**
		nous	**saurions**
		vous	**sauriez**
		ils	**sauraient**

PAST HISTORIC		PRESENT SUBJUNCTIVE	
je	sus	je	sache
tu	sus	tu	saches
il	sut	il	sache
nous	sûmes	nous	sachions
vous	sûtes	vous	sachiez
ils	surent	ils	sachent

PERFECT		PAST SUBJUNCTIVE	
j'	ai su	je	susse
tu	as su	tu	susses
il	a su	il	sût
nous	avons su	nous	sussions
vous	avez su	vous	sussiez
ils	ont su	ils	sussent

CONSTRUCTIONS

savoir faire   to know how to do; to be able to do
je ne sais pas quoi faire   I don't know what to do
je vous ferai savoir   I'll let you know
à savoir   that is, namely
on ne sait jamais   you never can tell

92 sentir

to smell; to feel   *also* **consentir**
                         to agree

PRESENT PARTICIPLE
sentant   **démentir**
                              to deny

PAST PARTICIPLE
senti   **mentir**
                              to lie

PRESENT		IMPERFECT	
je	**sens**	je	**sent**ais
tu	**sens**	tu	**sent**ais
il	**sent**	il	**sent**ait
nous	**sent**ons	nous	**sent**ions
vous	**sent**ez	vous	**sent**iez
ils	**sent**ent	ils	**sent**aient

FUTURE

je	**sent**irai
tu	**sent**iras
il	**sent**ira
nous	**sent**irons
vous	**sent**irez
ils	**sent**iront

IMPERATIVE	CONDITIONAL	
sens	je	**sent**irais
sentons	tu	**sent**irais
sentez	il	**sent**irait
	nous	**sent**irions
	vous	**sent**iriez
	ils	**sent**iraient

ressentir
to feel

PAST HISTORIC
je	**sent**is
tu	**sent**is
il	**sent**it
nous	**sent**îmes
vous	**sent**îtes
ils	**sent**irent

PERFECT
j'	**ai sent**i
tu	**as sent**i
il	**a sent**i
nous	**avons sent**i
vous	**avez sent**i
ils	**ont sent**i

PRESENT SUBJUNCTIVE
je	**sent**e
tu	**sent**es
il	**sent**e
nous	**sent**ions
vous	**sent**iez
ils	**sent**ent

PAST SUBJUNCTIVE
je	**sent**isse
tu	**sent**isses
il	**sent**ît
nous	**sent**issions
vous	**sent**issiez
ils	**sent**issent

CONSTRUCTIONS
sentir bon/mauvais to smell good *or* nice/bad
j'ai senti s'arrêter la voiture I felt the car stopping
se sentir mal/mieux to feel ill/better

93 servir

to serve

PRESENT PARTICIPLE
servant

PAST PARTICIPLE
servi

PRESENT		*IMPERFECT*	
je	**sers**	je	**servais**
tu	**sers**	tu	**servais**
il	**sert**	il	**servait**
nous	**servons**	nous	**servions**
vous	**servez**	vous	**serviez**
ils	**servent**	ils	**servaient**

		FUTURE	
		je	**servirai**
		tu	**serviras**
		il	**servira**
		nous	**servirons**
		vous	**servirez**
		ils	**serviront**

IMPERATIVE	*CONDITIONAL*	
sers	je	**servirais**
servons	tu	**servirais**
servez	il	**servirait**
	nous	**servirions**
	vous	**serviriez**
	ils	**serviraient**

PAST HISTORIC		PRESENT SUBJUNCTIVE	
je	**serv**is	je	**serv**e
tu	**serv**is	tu	**serv**es
il	**serv**it	il	**serv**e
nous	**serv**îmes	nous	**serv**ions
vous	**serv**îtes	vous	**serv**iez
ils	**serv**irent	ils	**serv**ent

PERFECT		PAST SUBJUNCTIVE	
j'	**ai serv**i	je	**serv**isse
tu	**as serv**i	tu	**serv**isses
il	**a serv**i	il	**serv**ît
nous	**avons serv**i	nous	**serv**issions
vous	**avez serv**i	vous	**serv**issiez
ils	**ont serv**i	ils	**serv**issent

CONSTRUCTIONS

servir un plat à qn   to serve sb with a dish
servir à qn/à qch   to be useful to sb/for sth
servir à faire   to be used for doing
à quoi sert de pleurer?   what's the use of crying?
servir de   to act as; to serve as
se servir d'un plat   to help oneself to a dish

94 songer
to think

also **plonger**
to dive

PRESENT PARTICIPLE
songeant

prolonger
to prolong

PAST PARTICIPLE
songé

rallonger
to lengthen

PRESENT
je	**songe**
tu	**songes**
il	**songe**
nous	**songeons**
vous	**songez**
ils	**songent**

IMPERFECT
je	**songeais**
tu	**songeais**
il	**songeait**
nous	**songions**
vous	**songiez**
ils	**songeaient**

FUTURE
je	**songerai**
tu	**songeras**
il	**songera**
nous	**songerons**
vous	**songerez**
ils	**songeront**

IMPERATIVE
songe
songeons
songez

CONDITIONAL
je	**songerais**
tu	**songerais**
il	**songerait**
nous	**songerions**
vous	**songeriez**
ils	**songeraient**

to think

ronger
to gnaw

PAST HISTORIC

je	**songeai**
tu	**songeas**
il	**songea**
nous	**songeâmes**
vous	**songeâtes**
ils	**songèrent**

PRESENT SUBJUNCTIVE

je	**songe**
tu	**songes**
il	**songe**
nous	**songions**
vous	**songiez**
ils	**songent**

PERFECT

j'	**ai songé**
tu	**as songé**
il	**a songé**
nous	**avons songé**
vous	**avez songé**
ils	**ont songé**

PAST SUBJUNCTIVE

je	**songeasse**
tu	**songeasses**
il	**songeât**
nous	**songeassions**
vous	**songeassiez**
ils	**songeassent**

CONSTRUCTIONS

songer à qch to think sth over; to think of sth
songer à faire qch to contemplate doing sth

95 sortir

to go out   *also* **ressortir**

to stand out

PRESENT PARTICIPLE
sortant

PAST PARTICIPLE
sorti

PRESENT		*IMPERFECT*	
je	**sors**	je	**sort**ais
tu	**sors**	tu	**sort**ais
il	**sort**	il	**sort**ait
nous	**sort**ons	nous	**sort**ions
vous	**sort**ez	vous	**sort**iez
ils	**sort**ent	ils	**sort**aient

		FUTURE	
		je	**sort**irai
		tu	**sort**iras
		il	**sort**ira
		nous	**sort**irons
		vous	**sort**irez
		ils	**sort**iront

IMPERATIVE		*CONDITIONAL*	
	sors	je	**sort**irais
	sortons	tu	**sort**irais
	sortez	il	**sort**irait
		nous	**sort**irions
		vous	**sort**iriez
		ils	**sort**iraient

PAST HISTORIC		PRESENT SUBJUNCTIVE	
je	**sortis**	je	**sorte**
tu	**sortis**	tu	**sortes**
il	**sortit**	il	**sorte**
nous	**sortîmes**	nous	**sortions**
vous	**sortîtes**	vous	**sortiez**
ils	**sortirent**	ils	**sortent**

PERFECT		PAST SUBJUNCTIVE	
je	**suis sorti**	je	**sortisse**
tu	**es sorti**	tu	**sortisses**
il	**est sorti**	il	**sortît**
nous	**sommes sortis**	nous	**sortissions**
vous	**êtes sorti(s)**	vous	**sortissiez**
ils	**sont sortis**	ils	**sortissent**

CONSTRUCTIONS

sortir d'une pièce/d'un pays to go (*or* come) out of a
room/leave a country
il a sorti la voiture du garage he got the car out of the
garage
sortir le chien to take the dog out

96 se souvenir
to remember

PRESENT PARTICIPLE
se souvenant

PAST PARTICIPLE
souvenu

PRESENT		*IMPERFECT*	
je	**me souviens**	je	**me souven**ais
tu	**te souviens**	tu	**te souven**ais
il	**se souvient**	il	**se souven**ait
nous	**nous souven**ons	nous	**nous souven**ions
vous	**vous souven**ez	vous	**vous souven**iez
ils	**se souviennent**	ils	**se souven**aient

		FUTURE	
		je	**me souviendr**ai
		tu	**te souviendr**as
		il	**se souviendr**a
		nous	**nous souviendr**ons
		vous	**vous souviendr**ez
		ils	**se souviendr**ont

IMPERATIVE	*CONDITIONAL*	
souviens-toi	je	**me souviendr**ais
souvenons-**nous**	tu	**te souviendr**ais
souvenez-**vous**	il	**se souviendr**ait
	nous	**nous souviendr**ions
	vous	**vous souviendr**iez
	ils	**se souviendr**aient

PAST HISTORIC		*PRESENT SUBJUNCTIVE*	
je	**me souvins**	je	**me souvienne**
tu	**te souvins**	tu	**te souviennes**
il	**se souvint**	il	**se souvienne**
nous	**nous souvînmes**	nous	**nous souvenions**
vous	**vous souvîntes**	vous	**vous souveniez**
ils	**se souvinrent**	ils	**se souviennent**
PERFECT		*PAST SUBJUNCTIVE*	
je	**me suis souvenu**	je	**me souvinsse**
tu	**t'es souvenu**	tu	**te souvinsses**
il	**s'est souvenu**	il	**se souvînt**
nous	**nous sommes souvenus**	nous	**nous souvinssions**
vous	**vous êtes souvenu(s)**	vous	**vous souvinssiez**
ils	**se sont souvenus**	ils	**se souvinssent**

CONSTRUCTIONS
se souvenir de qn/qch   to remember sb/sth
se souvenir d'avoir fait qch   to remember doing sth

97 suffire

to be enough

PRESENT PARTICIPLE
suffisant

PAST PARTICIPLE
suffi

PRESENT		IMPERFECT	
je	**suffis**	je	**suffisais**
tu	**suffis**	tu	**suffisais**
il	**suffit**	il	**suffisait**
nous	**suffisons**	nous	**suffisions**
vous	**suffisez**	vous	**suffisiez**
ils	**suffisent**	ils	**suffisaient**

		FUTURE	
		je	**suffirai**
		tu	**suffiras**
		il	**suffira**
		nous	**suffirons**
		vous	**suffirez**
		ils	**suffiront**

IMPERATIVE	CONDITIONAL	
suffis	je	**suffirais**
suffisons	tu	**suffirais**
suffisez	il	**suffirait**
	nous	**suffirions**
	vous	**suffiriez**
	ils	**suffiraient**

PAST HISTORIC		PRESENT SUBJUNCTIVE	
je	**suffis**	je	**suffise**
tu	**suffis**	tu	**suffises**
il	**suffit**	il	**suffise**
nous	**suffîmes**	nous	**suffisions**
vous	**suffîtes**	vous	**suffisiez**
ils	**suffirent**	ils	**suffisent**

PERFECT		PAST SUBJUNCTIVE	
j'	**ai suffi**	je	**suffisse**
tu	**as suffi**	tu	**suffisses**
il	**a suffi**	il	**suffît**
nous	**avons suffi**	nous	**suffissions**
vous	**avez suffi**	vous	**suffissiez**
ils	**ont suffi**	ils	**suffissent**

CONSTRUCTIONS

suffire à *or* **pour faire**   to be sufficient *or* enough to do
suffire à qn   to be enough for sb
(ça) suffit!   that's enough!, that will do!
il suffit de 2 heures pour y aller   2 hours is enough to get there

98 suivre
to follow   *also* **poursuivre**
                  to pursue

PRESENT PARTICIPLE
suivant

PAST PARTICIPLE
suivi

PRESENT	*IMPERFECT*
je **suis**	je **suiv**ais
tu **suis**	tu **suiv**ais
il **suit**	il **suiv**ait
nous **suiv**ons	nous **suiv**ions
vous **suiv**ez	vous **suiv**iez
ils **suiv**ent	ils **suiv**aient

	FUTURE
	je **suiv**rai
	tu **suiv**ras
	il **suiv**ra
	nous **suiv**rons
	vous **suiv**rez
	ils **suiv**ront

IMPERATIVE	*CONDITIONAL*
suis	je **suiv**rais
suivons	tu **suiv**rais
suivez	il **suiv**rait
	nous **suiv**rions
	vous **suiv**riez
	ils **suiv**raient

PAST HISTORIC		PRESENT SUBJUNCTIVE	
je	**suivis**	je	**suive**
tu	**suivis**	tu	**suives**
il	**suivit**	il	**suive**
nous	**suivîmes**	nous	**suivions**
vous	**suivîtes**	vous	**suiviez**
ils	**suivirent**	ils	**suivent**

PERFECT		PAST SUBJUNCTIVE	
j'	**ai suivi**	je	**suivisse**
tu	**as suivi**	tu	**suivisses**
il	**a suivi**	il	**suivît**
nous	**avons suivi**	nous	**suivissions**
vous	**avez suivi**	vous	**suivissiez**
ils	**ont suivi**	ils	**suivissent**

CONSTRUCTIONS

suivre un régime   to be on a diet
suivre une classe   to attend a class
faire suivre son courrier   to have one's mail forwarded

99 surseoir

to defer

PRESENT PARTICIPLE
sursoyant

PAST PARTICIPLE
sursis

PRESENT		IMPERFECT	
je	**surs**ois	je	**surs**oyais
tu	**surs**ois	tu	**surs**oyais
il	**surs**oit	il	**surs**oyait
nous	**surs**oyons	nous	**surs**oyions
vous	**surs**oyez	vous	**surs**oyiez
ils	**surs**oient	ils	**surs**oyaient

		FUTURE	
		je	**surseoir**ai
		tu	**surseoir**as
		il	**surseoir**a
		nous	**surseoir**ons
		vous	**surseoir**ez
		ils	**surseoir**ont

IMPERATIVE	CONDITIONAL	
sursois	je	**surseoir**ais
sursoyons	tu	**surseoir**ais
sursoyez	il	**surseoir**ait
	nous	**surseoir**ions
	vous	**surseoir**iez
	ils	**surseoir**aient

to defer

PAST HISTORIC		*PRESENT SUBJUNCTIVE*	
je	**surs**is	je	**surs**oie
tu	**surs**is	tu	**surs**oies
il	**surs**it	il	**surs**oie
nous	**surs**îmes	nous	**surs**oyions
vous	**surs**îtes	vous	**surs**oyiez
ils	**surs**irent	ils	**surs**oient
PERFECT		*PAST SUBJUNCTIVE*	
j'	**ai surs**is	je	**surs**isse
tu	**as surs**is	tu	**surs**isses
il	**a surs**is	il	**surs**ît
nous	**avons surs**is	nous	**surs**issions
vous	**avez surs**is	vous	**surs**issiez
ils	**ont surs**is	ils	**surs**issent

CONSTRUCTIONS

surseoir à qch   to defer *or* postpone sth

100 se taire

to stop talking

PRESENT PARTICIPLE
se taisant

PAST PARTICIPLE
tu

PRESENT

je	**me tais**
tu	**te tais**
il	**se tait**
nous	**nous taisons**
vous	**vous taisez**
ils	**se taisent**

IMPERATIVE

tais-toi
taisons-nous
taisez-vous

IMPERFECT

je	**me taisais**
tu	**te taisais**
il	**se taisait**
nous	**nous taisions**
vous	**vous taisiez**
ils	**se taisaient**

FUTURE

je	**me tairai**
tu	**te tairas**
il	**se taira**
nous	**nous tairons**
vous	**vous tairez**
ils	**se tairont**

CONDITIONAL

je	**me tairais**
tu	**te tairais**
il	**se tairait**
nous	**nous tairions**
vous	**vous tairiez**
ils	**se tairaient**

to stop talking

PAST HISTORIC		PRESENT SUBJUNCTIVE	
je	**me tus**	je	**me taise**
tu	**te tus**	tu	**te taises**
il	**se tut**	il	**se taise**
nous	**nous tûmes**	nous	**nous taisions**
vous	**vous tûtes**	vous	**vous taisiez**
ils	**se turent**	ils	**se taisent**

PERFECT		PAST SUBJUNCTIVE	
je	**me suis tu**	je	**me tusse**
tu	**t'es tu**	tu	**te tusses**
il	**s'est tu**	il	**se tût**
nous	**nous sommes tus**	nous	**nous tussions**
vous	**vous êtes tu(s)**	vous	**vous tussiez**
ils	**se sont tus**	ils	**se tussent**

CONSTRUCTIONS

ils se sont tus they stopped talking
taisez-vous! be quiet!
se taire sur qch to keep quiet about sth

101 tenir

to hold

also **appartenir**
to belong

PRESENT PARTICIPLE
tenant

contenir
to contain

PAST PARTICIPLE
tenu

entretenir
to maintain

PRESENT	
je	**tiens**
tu	**tiens**
il	**tient**
nous	**tenons**
vous	**tenez**
ils	**tiennent**

IMPERFECT	
je	**tenais**
tu	**tenais**
il	**tenait**
nous	**tenions**
vous	**teniez**
ils	**tenaient**

FUTURE	
je	**tiendrai**
tu	**tiendras**
il	**tiendra**
nous	**tiendrons**
vous	**tiendrez**
ils	**tiendront**

IMPERATIVE
tiens
tenons
tenez

CONDITIONAL	
je	**tiendrais**
tu	**tiendrais**
il	**tiendrait**
nous	**tiendrions**
vous	**tiendriez**
ils	**tiendraient**

soutenir
to support

to hold

PAST HISTORIC		PRESENT SUBJUNCTIVE	
je	tins	je	tienne
tu	tins	tu	tiennes
il	tint	il	tienne
nous	tînmes	nous	tenions
vous	tîntes	vous	teniez
ils	tinrent	ils	tiennent

PERFECT		PAST SUBJUNCTIVE	
j'	ai tenu	je	tinsse
tu	as tenu	tu	tinsses
il	a tenu	il	tînt
nous	avons tenu	nous	tinssions
vous	avez tenu	vous	tinssiez
ils	ont tenu	ils	tinssent

CONSTRUCTIONS
tenir à   to be attached to; to care about
tenir à faire   to be keen to do
il ne tient qu'à vous de décider   it's up to you to decide
se tenir   to stand; to take place
être tenu de faire   to be obliged to do

102 tomber

to fall

also **retomber**
to fall back

PRESENT PARTICIPLE
tombant

PAST PARTICIPLE
tombé

PRESENT		IMPERFECT	
je	**tombe**	je	**tombais**
tu	**tombes**	tu	**tombais**
il	**tombe**	il	**tombait**
nous	**tombons**	nous	**tombions**
vous	**tombez**	vous	**tombiez**
ils	**tombent**	ils	**tombaient**

FUTURE	
je	**tomberai**
tu	**tomberas**
il	**tombera**
nous	**tomberons**
vous	**tomberez**
ils	**tomberont**

IMPERATIVE	CONDITIONAL	
tombe	je	**tomberais**
tombons	tu	**tomberais**
tombez	il	**tomberait**
	nous	**tomberions**
	vous	**tomberiez**
	ils	**tomberaient**

PAST HISTORIC		PRESENT SUBJUNCTIVE	
je	**tombai**	je	**tombe**
tu	**tombas**	tu	**tombes**
il	**tomba**	il	**tombe**
nous	**tombâmes**	nous	**tombions**
vous	**tombâtes**	vous	**tombiez**
ils	**tombèrent**	ils	**tombent**

PERFECT		PAST SUBJUNCTIVE	
je	**suis tombé**	je	**tombasse**
tu	**es tombé**	tu	**tombasses**
il	**est tombé**	il	**tombât**
nous	**sommes tombés**	nous	**tombassions**
vous	**êtes tombé(s)**	vous	**tombassiez**
ils	**sont tombés**	ils	**tombassent**

CONSTRUCTIONS
tomber de bicyclette/cheval   to fall off one's
bicycle/horse
laisser tomber qch   to drop sth
faire tomber   to knock over; to knock down
tomber malade/amoureux   to fall ill/in love
tomber sur   to come across

103 traduire
to translate

PRESENT PARTICIPLE
traduisant

PAST PARTICIPLE
traduit

PRESENT		IMPERFECT	
je	**tradui**s	je	**tradui**sais
tu	**tradui**s	tu	**tradui**sais
il	**tradui**t	il	**tradui**sait
nous	**tradui**sons	nous	**tradui**sions
vous	**tradui**sez	vous	**tradui**siez
ils	**tradui**sent	ils	**tradui**saient

FUTURE	
je	**traduir**ai
tu	**traduir**as
il	**traduir**a
nous	**traduir**ons
vous	**traduir**ez
ils	**traduir**ont

IMPERATIVE	CONDITIONAL	
traduis	je	**traduir**ais
traduisons	tu	**traduir**ais
traduisez	il	**traduir**ait
	nous	**traduir**ions
	vous	**traduir**iez
	ils	**traduir**aient

PAST HISTORIC		PRESENT SUBJUNCTIVE	
je	traduisis	je	traduise
tu	traduisis	tu	traduises
il	traduisit	il	traduise
nous	traduisîmes	nous	traduisions
vous	traduisîtes	vous	traduisiez
ils	traduisirent	ils	traduisent

PERFECT		PAST SUBJUNCTIVE	
j'	ai traduit	je	traduisisse
tu	as traduit	tu	traduisisses
il	a traduit	il	traduisît
nous	avons traduit	nous	traduisissions
vous	avez traduit	vous	traduisissiez
ils	ont traduit	ils	traduisissent

CONSTRUCTIONS

traduit en/du français translated into/from French

104 traire

to milk

also distraire
to distract

PRESENT PARTICIPLE
trayant

extraire
to extract

PAST PARTICIPLE
trait

soustraire
to subtract

PRESENT
je	**trais**
tu	**trais**
il	**trait**
nous	trayons
vous	trayez
ils	**traient**

IMPERFECT
je	trayais
tu	trayais
il	trayait
nous	trayions
vous	trayiez
ils	trayaient

FUTURE
je	**trairai**
tu	**trairas**
il	**traira**
nous	**trairons**
vous	**trairez**
ils	**trairont**

IMPERATIVE
	trais
	trayons
	trayez

CONDITIONAL
je	**trairais**
tu	**trairais**
il	**trairait**
nous	**trairions**
vous	**trairiez**
ils	**trairaient**

PAST HISTORIC	PRESENT SUBJUNCTIVE
not used	je **traie**
	tu **traies**
	il **traie**
	nous **trayions**
	vous **trayiez**
	ils **traient**

PERFECT	PAST SUBJUNCTIVE
j' **ai trait**	*not used*
tu **as trait**	
il **a trait**	
nous **avons trait**	
vous **avez trait**	
ils **ont trait**	

105 vaincre
to defeat *also* **convaincre**
to convince

PRESENT PARTICIPLE
vainquant

PAST PARTICIPLE
vaincu

PRESENT		IMPERFECT	
je	**vaincs**	je	**vainquais**
tu	**vaincs**	tu	**vainquais**
il	**vainc**	il	**vainquait**
nous	**vainquons**	nous	**vainquions**
vous	**vainquez**	vous	**vainquiez**
ils	**vainquent**	ils	**vainquaient**

FUTURE	
je	**vaincrai**
tu	**vaincras**
il	**vaincra**
nous	**vaincrons**
vous	**vaincrez**
ils	**vaincront**

IMPERATIVE	CONDITIONAL	
vaincs	je	**vaincrais**
vainquons	tu	**vaincrais**
vainquez	il	**vaincrait**
	nous	**vaincrions**
	vous	**vaincriez**
	ils	**vaincraient**

PAST HISTORIC		PRESENT SUBJUNCTIVE	
je	**vainquis**	je	**vainque**
tu	**vainquis**	tu	**vainques**
il	**vainquit**	il	**vainque**
nous	**vainquîmes**	nous	**vainquions**
vous	**vainquîtes**	vous	**vainquiez**
ils	**vainquirent**	ils	**vainquent**

PERFECT		PAST SUBJUNCTIVE	
j'	**ai vaincu**	je	**vainquisse**
tu	**as vaincu**	tu	**vainquisses**
il	**a vaincu**	il	**vainquît**
nous	**avons vaincu**	nous	**vainquissions**
vous	**avez vaincu**	vous	**vainquissiez**
ils	**ont vaincu**	ils	**vainquissent**

CONSTRUCTIONS
s'avouer vaincu   to admit defeat

106 valoir
to be worth

PRESENT PARTICIPLE
valant

PAST PARTICIPLE
valu

PRESENT	*IMPERFECT*
je **vaux**	je **val**ais
tu **vaux**	tu **val**ais
il **vaut**	il **val**ait
nous **val**ons	nous **val**ions
vous **val**ez	vous **val**iez
ils **val**ent	ils **val**aient

	FUTURE
	je **vaudrai**
	tu **vaudras**
	il **vaudra**
	nous **vaudrons**
	vous **vaudrez**
	ils **vaudront**

IMPERATIVE	*CONDITIONAL*
vaux	je **vaudrais**
valons	tu **vaudrais**
valez	il **vaudrait**
	nous **vaudrions**
	vous **vaudriez**
	ils **vaudraient**

PAST HISTORIC		PRESENT SUBJUNCTIVE	
je	**valus**	je	**vaille**
tu	**valus**	tu	**vailles**
il	**valut**	il	**vaille**
nous	**valûmes**	nous	**valions**
vous	**valûtes**	vous	**valiez**
ils	**valurent**	ils	**vaillent**

PERFECT		PAST SUBJUNCTIVE	
j'	**ai valu**	je	**valusse**
tu	**as valu**	tu	**valusses**
il	**a valu**	il	**valût**
nous	**avons valu**	nous	**valussions**
vous	**avez valu**	vous	**valussiez**
ils	**ont valu**	ils	**valussent**

CONSTRUCTIONS

valoir cher / 10 F to be worth a lot / 10 F
cet outil ne vaut rien this tool is useless
il vaut mieux se taire it's better to say nothing
ce film vaut la peine d'être vu this film is worth seeing

107 vendre

to sell

also **défendre**
to defend

PRESENT PARTICIPLE
vendant

dépendre
to depend

PAST PARTICIPLE
vendu

entendre
to hear

PRESENT

je	**vend**s
tu	**vend**s
il	**vend**
nous	**vend**ons
vous	**vend**ez
ils	**vend**ent

IMPERFECT

je	**vend**ais
tu	**vend**ais
il	**vend**ait
nous	**vend**ions
vous	**vend**iez
ils	**vend**aient

FUTURE

je	**vend**rai
tu	**vend**ras
il	**vend**ra
nous	**vend**rons
vous	**vend**rez
ils	**vend**ront

IMPERATIVE

vends
vendons
vendez

CONDITIONAL

je	**vend**rais
tu	**vend**rais
il	**vend**rait
nous	**vend**rions
vous	**vend**riez
ils	**vend**raient

to sell

pendre
to hang

répandre
to spread

tendre
to stretch

PAST HISTORIC		PRESENT SUBJUNCTIVE	
je	**vendis**	je	**vende**
tu	**vendis**	tu	**vendes**
il	**vendit**	il	**vende**
nous	**vendîmes**	nous	**vendions**
vous	**vendîtes**	vous	**vendiez**
ils	**vendirent**	ils	**vendent**

PERFECT		PAST SUBJUNCTIVE	
j'	**ai vendu**	je	**vendisse**
tu	**as vendu**	tu	**vendisses**
il	**a vendu**	il	**vendît**
nous	**avons vendu**	nous	**vendissions**
vous	**avez vendu**	vous	**vendissiez**
ils	**ont vendu**	ils	**vendissent**

CONSTRUCTIONS

vendre qch à qn   to sell sb sth
il me l'a vendu 10 F   he sold it to me for 10 F
'à vendre'   'for sale'
ils se vendent à la pièce/douzaine   they are sold
singly/by the dozen

108 venir

to come

also intervenir
to intervene

PRESENT PARTICIPLE
venant

parvenir
to succeed

PAST PARTICIPLE
venu

survenir
to occur

PRESENT		*IMPERFECT*	
je	**viens**	je	**ven**ais
tu	**viens**	tu	**ven**ais
il	**vient**	il	**ven**ait
nous	**ven**ons	nous	**ven**ions
vous	**ven**ez	vous	**ven**iez
ils	**vien**nent	ils	**ven**aient

		FUTURE	
		je	**viendr**ai
		tu	**viendr**as
		il	**viendr**a
		nous	**viendr**ons
		vous	**viendr**ez
		ils	**viendr**ont

IMPERATIVE		*CONDITIONAL*	
	viens	je	**viendr**ais
	venons	tu	**viendr**ais
	venez	il	**viendr**ait
		nous	**viendr**ions
		vous	**viendr**iez
		ils	**viendr**aient

228

PAST HISTORIC		PRESENT SUBJUNCTIVE	
je	vins	je	vienne
tu	vins	tu	viennes
il	vint	il	vienne
nous	vînmes	nous	venions
vous	vîntes	vous	veniez
ils	vinrent	ils	viennent

PERFECT		PAST SUBJUNCTIVE	
je	suis venu	je	vinsse
tu	es venu	tu	vinsses
il	est venu	il	vînt
nous	sommes venus	nous	vinssions
vous	êtes venu(s)	vous	vinssiez
ils	sont venus	ils	vinssent

CONSTRUCTIONS

venir de Paris   to come from Paris
faire venir qn   to call *or* send for sb
venir de faire qch   to have just done sth
en venir à faire qch   to be reduced to doing sth

109 vêtir

to dress   *also* **revêtir**

to put on

PRESENT PARTICIPLE
vêtant

PAST PARTICIPLE
vêtu

PRESENT		IMPERFECT	
je	**vêts**	je	**vêtais**
tu	**vêts**	tu	**vêtais**
il	**vêt**	il	**vêtait**
nous	**vêtons**	nous	**vêtions**
vous	**vêtez**	vous	**vêtiez**
ils	**vêtent**	ils	**vêtaient**

FUTURE

je	**vêtirai**
tu	**vêtiras**
il	**vêtira**
nous	**vêtirons**
vous	**vêtirez**
ils	**vêtiront**

IMPERATIVE	CONDITIONAL	
vêts	je	**vêtirais**
vêtons	tu	**vêtirais**
vêtez	il	**vêtirait**
	nous	**vêtirions**
	vous	**vêtiriez**
	ils	**vêtiraient**

PAST HISTORIC		PRESENT SUBJUNCTIVE	
je	**vêtis**	je	**vête**
tu	**vêtis**	tu	**vêtes**
il	**vêtit**	il	**vête**
nous	**vêtîmes**	nous	**vêtions**
vous	**vêtîtes**	vous	**vêtiez**
ils	**vêtirent**	ils	**vêtent**

PERFECT		PAST SUBJUNCTIVE	
j'	**ai vêtu**	je	**vêtisse**
tu	**as vêtu**	tu	**vêtisses**
il	**a vêtu**	il	**vêtît**
nous	**avons vêtu**	nous	**vêtissions**
vous	**avez vêtu**	vous	**vêtissiez**
ils	**ont vêtu**	ils	**vêtissent**

CONSTRUCTIONS

vêtu d'un pantalon et d'un chandail wearing trousers and a sweater

se vêtir to dress

110 vivre

to live — *also* **survivre**
to survive

PRESENT PARTICIPLE
vivant

PAST PARTICIPLE
vécu

PRESENT		*IMPERFECT*	
je	**vis**	je	**viv**ais
tu	**vis**	tu	**viv**ais
il	**vit**	il	**viv**ait
nous	**vivons**	nous	**vivions**
vous	**vivez**	vous	**viviez**
ils	**vivent**	ils	**vivaient**

		FUTURE	
		je	**vivr**ai
		tu	**vivr**as
		il	**vivr**a
		nous	**vivrons**
		vous	**vivrez**
		ils	**vivront**

IMPERATIVE		*CONDITIONAL*	
	vis	je	**vivr**ais
	vivons	tu	**vivr**ais
	vivez	il	**vivr**ait
		nous	**vivrions**
		vous	**vivriez**
		ils	**vivraient**

PAST HISTORIC		PRESENT SUBJUNCTIVE	
je	**véc**us	je	**vive**
tu	**véc**us	tu	**vive**s
il	**véc**ut	il	**vive**
nous	**véc**ûmes	nous	**viv**ions
vous	**véc**ûtes	vous	**viv**iez
ils	**véc**urent	ils	**vive**nt

PERFECT		PAST SUBJUNCTIVE	
j'	**ai** vécu	je	**véc**usse
tu	**as** vécu	tu	**véc**usses
il	**a** vécu	il	**véc**ût
nous	**avons** vécu	nous	**véc**ussions
vous	**avez** vécu	vous	**véc**ussiez
ils	**ont** vécu	ils	**véc**ussent

CONSTRUCTIONS
il vit à la campagne/en France he lives in the country/in France
vivre de rentes/légumes to live on a private income/on vegetables
il est facile/difficile à vivre he's easy/difficult to get on with

111 voir

to see

also **entrevoir**
to catch a glimpse of

PRESENT PARTICIPLE
voyant

revoir
to revise

PAST PARTICIPLE
vu

PRESENT
je	**vois**
tu	**vois**
il	**voit**
nous	**voyons**
vous	**voyez**
ils	**voient**

IMPERFECT
je	voyais
tu	voyais
il	voyait
nous	voyions
vous	voyiez
ils	voyaient

FUTURE
je	verrai
tu	verras
il	verra
nous	verrons
vous	verrez
ils	verront

IMPERATIVE
vois
voyons
voyez

CONDITIONAL
je	verrais
tu	verrais
il	verrait
nous	verrions
vous	verriez
ils	verraient

PAST HISTORIC		PRESENT SUBJUNCTIVE	
je	vis	je	voie
tu	vis	tu	voies
il	vit	il	voie
nous	vîmes	nous	voyions
vous	vîtes	vous	voyiez
ils	virent	ils	voient

PERFECT		PAST SUBJUNCTIVE	
j'	ai vu	je	visse
tu	as vu	tu	visses
il	a vu	il	vît
nous	avons vu	nous	vissions
vous	avez vu	vous	vissiez
ils	ont vu	ils	vissent

CONSTRUCTIONS

aller voir qn   to go and see sb
faire voir qch   to show sth
on verra bien   we'll soon see
ça n'a rien à voir avec notre problème   it's got nothing to do with our problem
voyons!   come now!

112 vouloir
to want

PRESENT PARTICIPLE
voulant

PAST PARTICIPLE
voulu

PRESENT		*IMPERFECT*	
je	**veux**	je	**voul**ais
tu	**veux**	tu	**voul**ais
il	**veut**	il	**voul**ait
nous	**voul**ons	nous	**voul**ions
vous	**voul**ez	vous	**voul**iez
ils	**veul**ent	ils	**voul**aient

		FUTURE	
		je	**voudr**ai
		tu	**voudr**as
		il	**voudr**a
		nous	**voudr**ons
		vous	**voudr**ez
		ils	**voudr**ont

IMPERATIVE	*CONDITIONAL*	
veuille	je	**voudr**ais
veuillons	tu	**voudr**ais
veuillez	il	**voudr**ait
	nous	**voudr**ions
	vous	**voudr**iez
	ils	**voudr**aient

PAST HISTORIC		PRESENT SUBJUNCTIVE	
je	**voulus**	je	**veuille**
tu	**voulus**	tu	**veuilles**
il	**voulut**	il	**veuille**
nous	**voulûmes**	nous	**voulions**
vous	**voulûtes**	vous	**vouliez**
ils	**voulurent**	ils	**veuillent**

PERFECT		PAST SUBJUNCTIVE	
j'	**ai voulu**	je	**voulusse**
tu	**as voulu**	tu	**voulusses**
il	**a voulu**	il	**voulût**
nous	**avons voulu**	nous	**voulussions**
vous	**avez voulu**	vous	**voulussiez**
ils	**ont voulu**	ils	**voulussent**

CONSTRUCTIONS

vouloir faire qch   to want to do sth
je veux bien le faire   I'm happy to do it; I don't mind doing it
en vouloir à qn   to have something against sb
vouloir dire   to mean

INDEX

(a) Each verb is numerically cross-referred to one of the 112 verb models shown in colour. Defective verbs, however, are cross-referred to page 13.

(b) All entries are arranged in alphabetical order; for alphabetisation purposes, pronouns are not included: s'asseoir, se taire etc appear as asseoir (s'), taire (se) etc.

(c) With the exception of those verbs which are individually marked (see note (d)), and of Reflexive and Reciprocal verbs which are always conjugated with être, a verb's auxiliary is that of its verb model.

(d) Superior numbers refer you to notes on page 256, which outline how the verb deviates from its verb model.

(e) An asterisk (*) indicates that the verb is conjugated with être when intransitive and avoir when transitive.

abaisser	36	accuser	36	aider	36
abandonner	36	acharner (s')	36	aigrir	45
abattre	11	acheminer	36	aiguiser	36
abêtir	45	**acheter**	1	aimanter	36
abîmer	36	achever	52	aimer	36
abolir	45	**acquérir**	2	ajouter	36
abonder	36	actionner	36	ajuster	36
abonner	36	activer	36	alarmer	36
aborder	36	adapter	36	alerter	36
aboutir	45	additionner	36	alimenter	36
aboyer	63	adhérer	41	allécher	41
abréger	80	adjoindre	51	alléger	80
abreuver	36	admettre	56	alléguer	41
abriter	36	admirer	36	**aller**	3
abrutir	45	adopter	36	allier	25
absenter (s')	36	adorer	36	allumer	36
absorber	36	adosser	36	altérer	41
absoudre[4]	85	adoucir	45	alterner	36
abstenir (s')	101	adresser	36	alunir	45
abstraire	104	advenir[3]	108	amaigrir	45
abuser	36	aérer	41	ambitionner	36
accabler	36	affaiblir	45	améliorer	36
accaparer	36	affairer (s')	36	aménager	54
accéder	41	affaisser (s')	36	amener	52
accélérer	41	affamer	36	ameuter	36
accepter	36	affermir	45	amincir	45
accompagner	36	afficher	36	amoindrir	45
accomplir	45	affirmer	36	amollir	45
accorder	36	affliger	54	amonceler	4
accoter	36	affoler	36	amorcer	15
accoucher	36	affranchir	45	amplifier	25
accouder (s')	36	affréter	41	amputer	36
accourir[5]	21	affronter	36	amuser	36
accoutumer	36	agacer	15	analyser	36
accrocher	36	agenouiller (s')	36	anéantir	45
accroire	*page 13*	agir	45	angoisser	36
accroître[6]	27	agiter	36	animer	36
accroupir (s')	45	agrandir	45	annexer	36
accueillir	28	agréer	24	annoncer	15
accumuler	36	ahurir	45	annoter	36

chuchoter	36	complimenter	36	constater	36
circoncire[8]	97	compliquer	36	consterner	36
circonscrire	38	comporter	36	constituer	36
circonvenir[1]	108	composer	36	construire	29
circuler	36	composter	36	consulter	36
cirer	36	**comprendre**	16	contacter	36
ciseler	1	compromettre	79	contaminer	36
citer	36	compter	36	contempler	36
clarifier	25	concéder	41	contenir	101
classer	36	concentrer	36	contenter	36
classifier	25	concerner	36	conter	36
cligner	36	concevoir	81	contester	36
clignoter	36	concilier	25	continuer	36
clore	14	**conclure**	17	contraindre	23
clouer	36	concourir	21	contrarier	25
coder	36	concurrencer	15	contraster	36
codifier	25	condamner	36	contredire	48
cogner	36	condenser	36	contrefaire	43
coiffer	36	condescendre[1]	31	contrevenir[1]	108
coincer	15	**conduire**	18	contribuer	36
coïncider	36	conférer	41	contrôler	36
collaborer	36	confier	25	convaincre	105
collectionner	36	confire[9]	97	convenir[1]	108
coller	36	confirmer	36	convertir	45
coloniser	36	confisquer	36	convier	25
colorer	36	confondre	84	convoquer	36
colorier	25	conforter	36	coopérer	41
combattre	11	congédier	25	copier	25
combler	36	congeler	1	correspondre	84
commander	36	**connaître**	19	corriger	54
commémorer	36	conquérir	2	corrompre	90
commencer	15	consacrer	36	corroyer	63
commettre	56	conseiller	36	côtoyer	63
communier	25	consentir	92	coucher	36
communiquer	36	considérer	41	**coudre**	20
comparaître	67	consister	36	couler	36
comparer	36	consoler	36	couper	36
compenser	36	consolider	36	courber	36
complaire	74	consommer	36	**courir**	21
compléter	41	conspirer	36	coûter	36

242

couvrir	22	déboutonner	36	décourager	54
cracher	36	débrailler (se)	36	**découvrir**	30
craindre	23	débrancher	36	décréter	41
craquer	36	débrayer	70	décrier	25
créer	24	débrouiller	36	décrire	38
crépir	45	débuter	36	décrocher	36
creuser	36	décaler	36	décroître[10]	27
crever	52	décanter	36	dédaigner	36
cribler	36	décaper	36	dédicacer	15
crier	25	décapoter	36	dédier	25
critiquer	36	décéder[2]	41	dédire	48
crocheter	1	déceler	1	dédommager	54
croire	26	décélérer	41	dédouaner	36
croiser	36	décentraliser	36	dédoubler	36
croître	27	décerner	36	déduire	29
crouler	36	décevoir	81	défaillir[11]	7
croupir	45	déchaîner	36	défaire	43
crucifier	25	décharger	54	défalquer	36
cueillir	28	déchiffrer	36	défavoriser	36
cuire	29	déchiqueter	50	défendre	107
culbuter	36	déchirer	36	déférer	41
cultiver	36	déchoir	*page 13*	déficeler	4
cumuler	36	décider	36	défier	25
curer	36	décimer	36	défigurer	36
daigner	36	déclamer	36	défiler	36
damner	36	déclarer	36	définir	45
danser	36	déclasser	36	défoncer	15
dater	36	déclencher	36	déformer	36
débarquer	36	décliner	36	défraîchir	45
débarrasser	36	décoder	36	dégager	54
débattre	11	décolérer	41	dégainer	36
débaucher	36	décoller	36	dégauchir	45
débiliter	36	décommander	36	dégazonner	36
débiter	36	déconcerter	36	dégeler	1
déblatérer	41	déconseiller	36	dégénérer	41
débloquer	36	décontracter	36	dégonfler	36
déboîter	36	décorer	36	dégourdir	45
déborder	36	découdre	20	dégoûter	36
déboucher	36	découler	36	dégrader	36
débourser	36	découper	36	dégringoler	36

dégriser	36	départager	54	désennuyer	63
déguerpir	45	départir (se)	68	désensibiliser	36
déguiser	36	dépasser	69	désentraver	36
déguster	36	dépayser	36	déséquilibrer	36
déjeter	50	dépecer	52	déserter	36
déjeuner	36	dépêcher	36	désespérer	41
déjouer	36	dépeindre	71	déshabiller	36
délaisser	36	dépendre	107	déshabituer	36
délayer	70	dépenser	36	déshériter	36
déléguer	41	dépérir	45	désigner	36
délibérer	41	dépister	36	désinfecter	36
délier	25	déplacer	15	désintégrer	41
délirer	36	déplaire	74	désintéresser	36
délivrer	36	déplier	25	désintoxiquer	36
déloger	54	déployer	63	désirer	36
demander	36	dépolir	45	désister (se)	36
démanteler	1	déposer	36	désobéir	45
démarquer	36	dépouiller	36	désoler	36
démarrer	36	dépoussiérer	41	désorganiser	36
démêler	36	déprécier	25	désorienter	36
déménager	54	déprendre	78	dessaisir	45
démener (se)	52	déprimer	36	dessécher	41
démentir	92	déraciner	36	desserrer	36
démettre	56	déranger	54	dessiner	36
demeurer[12]	36	déraper	36	destiner	36
démissionner	36	dérégler	41	destituer	36
démolir	45	déroger	54	désunir	45
démonter[1]	57	dérouler	36	détacher	36
démontrer	36	dérouter	36	détailler	36
démultiplier	25	désaccoutumer	36	détecter	36
démunir	45	désagréger	80	déteindre	71
dénaturer	36	désaltérer	41	dételer	4
dénier	25	désamorcer	15	détendre	107
dénigrer	36	désapprendre	5	détenir	101
déniveler	4	désapprouver	36	détériorer	36
dénombrer	36	désassortir	45	déterminer	36
dénoncer	15	désavantager	54	détester	36
dénouer	36	désavouer	36	détordre	58
dépanner	36	descendre*	31	détourner	36
dépaqueter	50	désemparer	36	détraquer	36

244

froncer	15	gravir	45	heurter	36
frotter	36	greffer	36	hocher	36
frustrer	36	grêler	36	honorer	36
fuir	46	griffonner	36	horrifier	25
fumer	36	grignoter	36	huer	36
fusiller	36	griller	36	humaniser	36
gâcher	36	grimacer	15	humidifier	25
gagner	36	grimper	36	humilier	25
galoper	36	grincer	15	hurler	36
garantir	45	griser	36	hypnotiser	36
garder	36	grogner	36	idéaliser	36
garer	36	grommeler	4	identifier	25
garnir	45	gronder	36	ignorer	36
gaspiller	36	grossir	45	illuminer	36
gâter	36	grouiller	36	illustrer	36
gauchir	45	grouper	36	imaginer	36
gaufrer	36	guérir	45	imiter	36
gausser (se)	36	guerroyer	63	immigrer	36
geindre	71	guetter	36	immiscer (s')	15
geler	1	guider	36	immobiliser	36
gémir	45	guinder	36	immoler	36
gêner	36	habiller	36	impatienter	36
généraliser	36	habiter	36	impliquer	36
gérer	41	habituer	36	implorer	36
gésir	*page 13*	hacher	36	importer	36
giboyer	63	haïr	47	impressionner	36
gifler	36	haleter	1	imprimer	36
givrer	36	handicaper	36	improviser	36
glacer	15	hanter	36	inaugurer	36
glisser	36	harceler	4	inciter	36
glorifier	25	harmoniser	36	incliner	36
gommer	36	hasarder	36	inclure[18]	17
gonfler	36	hâter	36	incommoder	36
goûter	36	hausser	36	incorporer	36
gouverner	36	héberger	54	incriminer	36
gracier	25	hébéter	41	inculper	36
grandir	45	hennir	45	indiquer	36
gratifier	25	hérisser	36	induire	29
gratter	36	hériter	36	infecter	36
graver	36	hésiter	36	infester	36

infirmer	36	invoquer	36	lorgner	36
infliger	54	irriter	36	lotir	45
influencer	15	isoler	36	loucher	36
informer	36	jaillir	45	louer	36
ingénier (s')	25	jaser	36	louper	36
inhaler	36	jaunir	45	louvoyer	63
initier	25	**jeter**	50	lubrifier	25
injurier	25	jeûner	36	lutter	36
innover	36	**joindre**	51	mâcher	36
inoculer	36	jouer	36	machiner	36
inonder	36	jouir	45	magnifier	25
inquiéter	41	juger	54	maigrir	45
inscrire	38	jumeler	4	maintenir	101
insensibiliser	36	jurer	36	maîtriser	36
insérer	41	justifier	25	majorer	36
insinuer	36	labourer	36	malfaire	43
insister	36	lacer	15	malmener	52
inspecter	36	lâcher	36	maltraiter	36
inspirer	36	laisser	36	**manger**	54
installer	36	lamenter (se)	36	manier	25
instituer	36	lancer	15	manifester	36
instruire	29	languir	45	manigancer	15
insulter	36	larmoyer	63	manipuler	36
insurger (s')	54	laver	36	manœuvrer	36
intégrer	41	lécher	41	manquer	36
intensifier	25	légaliser	36	manufacturer	36
intercéder	41	légiférer	41	manutentionner	36
interdire	48	lésiner	36	marcher	36
intéresser	36	**lever**	52	marier	25
interloquer	36	libérer	41	marquer	36
interroger	54	licencier	25	marteler	1
interrompre	90	lier	25	masquer	36
intervenir	108	ligoter	36	massacrer	36
intituler	36	limer	36	masser	36
intriguer	36	limiter	36	matérialiser	36
introduire	49	liquéfier	25	**maudire**	55
inventer	36	liquider	36	maugréer	24
invertir	45	**lire**	53	mécaniser	36
investir	45	livrer	36	méconnaître	19
inviter	36	loger	54	mécontenter	36

médire	48	mortifier	25	obliger	54
méditer	36	motiver	36	oblitérer	41
méfaire	43	moucher	36	obscurcir	45
méfier (se)	25	**moudre**	59	obséder	41
mélanger	54	mouiller	36	observer	36
mêler	36	**mourir**	60	obstiner (s')	36
menacer	15	**mouvoir**	61	**obtenir**	64
ménager	54	muer	36	occuper	36
mendier	25	multiplier	25	octroyer	63
mener	52	munir	45	offenser	36
mentionner	36	mûrir	45	**offrir**	65
mentir	92	murmurer	36	oindre	*page 13*
méprendre (se)	78	museler	4	omettre	56
mépriser	36	muter	36	opérer	41
mériter	36	mutiler	36	opposer	36
messeoir	*page 13*	mystifier	25	opprimer	36
mesurer	36	nager	54	ordonner	36
mettre	56	**naître**	62	organiser	36
meubler	36	nantir	45	orner	36
meugler	36	narrer	36	orthographier	25
meurtrir	45	naviguer	36	osciller	36
miauler	36	navrer	36	oser	36
mijoter	36	nécessiter	36	ôter	36
mimer	36	négliger	54	oublier	25
miner	36	négocier	25	ouïr	*page 13*
minimiser	36	neiger	54	outrager	54
mobiliser	36	**nettoyer**	63	**ouvrir**	66
modeler	1	nier	25	oxyder	36
modérer	41	niveler	4	pacifier	25
moderniser	36	noircir	45	paître	*page 13*
modifier	25	nommer	36	pâlir	45
moisir	45	normaliser	36	palper	36
moissonner	36	noter	36	palpiter	36
mollir	45	nouer	36	panser	36
monnayer	70	nourrir	45	parachever	52
monopoliser	36	noyer	63	parachuter	36
monter★	57	nuire[19]	29	**paraître**	67
montrer	36	numéroter	36	paralyser	36
moquer (se)	36	obéir	45	parcourir	21
mordre	58	objecter	36	pardonner	36

punir	45	rassembler	36	recueillir	28
purifier	25	rasséréner	41	recuire	29
qualifier	25	rassurer	36	reculer	36
quereller	36	rater	36	récupérer	41
questionner	36	rationaliser	36	recycler	36
quêter	36	rattraper	36	redescendre	31
quitter	36	ravir	45	rédiger	54
rabattre	11	ravitailler	36	redire	35
raccommoder	36	réagir	45	redoubler	36
raccompagner	36	réaliser	36	redouter	36
raccorder	36	rebattre	11	redresser	36
raccourcir	45	rebondir	45	réduire	29
raccrocher	36	rebuter	36	refaire	43
racheter	1	receler	1	référer	41
racler	36	recenser	36	refermer	36
racoler	36	recevoir	81	réfléchir	45
raconter	36	réchapper	36	refléter	41
raffermir	45	réchauffer	36	refondre	84
raffiner	36	rechercher	36	réformer	36
rafler	36	réciter	36	refroidir	45
rafraîchir	45	réclamer	36	réfugier (se)	25
ragaillardir	45	récolter	36	refuser	36
raidir	45	recommander	36	réfuter	36
railler	36	recommencer	15	regagner	36
raisonner	36	récompenser	36	regaillardir	45
rajeunir	45	réconcilier	25	regarder	36
rajouter	36	reconduire	18	régénérer	41
rajuster	36	réconforter	36	régir	45
ralentir	45	reconnaître	19	régler	41
rallier	25	reconquérir	2	régner	41
rallonger	94	reconstruire	29	regretter	36
rallumer	36	reconvertir	45	regrouper	36
ramasser	36	recopier	25	réhabiliter	36
ramener	52	recoudre	20	réhabituer	36
ramollir	45	recourir	21	rehausser	36
ranimer	36	recouvrir	22	réimprimer	36
rappeler	4	récréer	24	réintégrer	41
rapporter	36	récrier (se)	25	rejaillir	45
rapprocher	36	récrire	38	rejeter	50
raser	36	rectifier	25	rejoindre	51

tolérer	41	tricher	36	verdoyer	63
tomber	102	tricoter	36	vérifier	25
tondre	84	trier	25	vernir	45
tonner	36	triompher	36	verrouiller	36
tordre	58	tripoter	36	verser	36
torpiller	36	tromper	36	**vêtir**	109
tortiller	36	troquer	36	vexer	36
torturer	36	trotter	36	vibrer	36
toucher	36	troubler	36	vider	36
tourmenter	36	trouer	36	vieillir	45
tourner	36	trouver	36	violer	36
tournoyer	63	truffer	36	virer	36
tousser	36	truquer	36	viser	36
tracasser	36	tuer	36	visiter	36
tracer	15	tutoyer	63	visser	36
traduire	103	ulcérer	41	vitrifier	25
trahir	45	unifier	25	vitupérer	41
traîner	36	unir	45	vivifier	25
traire	104	urbaniser	36	**vivre**	110
traiter	36	user	36	vociférer	41
transcrire	38	usiner	36	voiler	36
transférer	41	utiliser	36	**voir**	111
transformer	36	vacciner	36	voler	36
transmettre	56	**vaincre**	105	vomir	45
transparaître	67	**valoir**	106	voter	36
transpirer	36	vanter	36	vouer	36
transplanter	36	varier	25	**vouloir**	112
transporter	36	végéter	41	vouvoyer	63
traquer	36	veiller	36	voyager	54
travailler	36	vendanger	54	vrombir	45
traverser	36	**vendre**	107	vulgariser	36
trébucher	36	venger	54	zébrer	41
trembler	36	**venir**	108	zézayer	70
tremper	36	verdir	45	zigzaguer	36

NOTES

1) *Auxiliary* = avoir.
2) *Auxiliary* = être.
3) *Only infinitive and 3rd persons of each tense used.*
4) *Past participle:* absous, absoute; *Past Historic and Past Subjunctive not used.*
5) *Conjugated with either* avoir *or* être.
6) *No circumflex on:* j'accrois, tu accrois, j'accrus, tu accrus, il accrut, ils accrurent, j'accrusse *etc,* accru.
7) *Hardly used except in infinitive and 3rd persons of Present, Future and Conditional.*
8) *Past participle:* circoncis.
9) *Past participle:* confit.
10) *As for* (6).
11) *Present tense singular, Future and Conditional tenses least common.*
12) *'To live': auxiliary* = avoir; *'to remain': auxiliary* = être.
13) *Past participle:* dissous, dissoute; *Past Historic and Past Subjunctive not used.*
14) *Auxiliary* = être; *NB:* il éclot; *hardly used except in 3rd persons.*
15) *Past participle:* ému.
16) *'To prosper': present participle* = florissant; *Imperfect* = florissait.
17) *Past participle:* frit; *used mainly in singular of Present tense and in compound tenses.*
18) *Past participle:* inclus.
19) *Past participle:* nui.
20) *In interrogative form,* 'puis' *is substituted for* 'peux': puis-je vous aider? = *may I help you?*
21) *Present Subjunctive:* je prévale *etc.*
22) *Future:* je prévoirai *etc; Conditional:* je prévoirais *etc.*
23) *Past participle:* promu; *used only in infinitive, both participles, and compound tenses.*
24) *Past participle:* relui; *Past Historic:* je reluis *etc.*
25) *No past participle – no compound tenses.*